GuardingKids.com

A Practical Guide to Keeping Kids Out of High-Tech Trouble

Russell A. Sabella, Ph.D.

GuardingKids.com

Copyright ©2008

Russell A. Sabella, Ph.D.

Library of Congress Control Number 2008926553

ISBN: 978-1-930572-55-3

Printing (Last Digit)

10 9 8 7 6 5 4 3 2 1

All rights reserved. No part of the material protected by this copyright notice may be reproduced or utilized in any form or by any means, electronic or mechanical, including photocopying, recording, or by any information storage and retrieval system, without the written permission of the copyright owner. Manufactured in the United States of America.

Publisher—

Educational Media Corporation®
P.O. Box 21311
Minneapolis, MN 55421-0311

(763) 781-0088 or (800) 966-3382

www.**educationalmedia**.com

Production editor—

Don L. Sorenson

Graphic design—

Earl Sorenson

Cover design—

Adquarters, Inc
Ft. Lauderdale, Florida

(954) 525-1901

www.adquarters.com

Contents

Dedication 6
Preface 6
    Evolution of GuardingKids.com 9
Chapter 1: Introduction **11**
    Where is the fence? 14
    The Bigger Picture 14
    Decisions... decisions... decisions 15
Chapter 2: A Web of Pornography, Prejudice, and More **17**
    Accidental Exposure: Pornography Plays Dirty 18
    Direct Access 20
    Basic Searching 20
        Basic Image Searches 21
        Basic Video Searches 22
    Advanced Web Searching 23
        File Type 23
        Directories 23
    Unsolicited E-mails 24
    Web Enabled Gadgets 24
    Other Inappropriate Websites 25
        Racism, Prejudice and Hate 25
        Self-Injury 26
        Eating Disorders 26
        Suicide 27
Chapter 3: High Tech Piracy **29**
    Downloading Music, Movies, and More 31
        Peer-to-Peer (P2P) File Sharing 32
        So what else should I know about downloading music? 33
    Cheating 34
        Cellphone cheating 34
        Online tools 34
        Gadgets 34
    Plagiarism 35
    Cracking Software Codes 36
    Counter-Cheating Technology 36
    What You Can Do 37

Chapter 4: Online Communication **39**
   Electronic Mail 39
      Potential Risk When Using E-mail 40
   I Want My Own E-mail Account! 41
   Chat Rooms 44
   Instant Messaging 45
   Video Communications 47
      Online Videos 47
   Telephony 48
   Blogs 49
      How Kids Create Their Own Blogs 49
   Podcasting 50
   Internet Social Networks 51
      So What's the Problem with Kids and Social Networking? 53
      Social Networking Safeguards 58
   Cyberbullying 59
      What to do if you suspect cyberbullying? 62
   Unanticipated Effects of Online Communication 64
   Cell Phones 65
      Text Messaging 66
      Cell Phone Distractions 67
      Mounting Minutes 68
      Cell Phones and Gaming 68
      Public Nuisance 69
      Cell Phones and Pornography 70
      Video Recording Trouble 71
      Win-Win Cell Phone Solutions 72

Chapter 5: Gaming **73**
   Positive Potential of Video Games 77
      Video Games and Physical Health 78
      Video Games and Learning 79
      Edutainment 80
      Video Games as the New "Third Place" 82
   Negative Potential of Video Games 83
      Violence and Desensitization 84
      Gaming Addictions 85
      Other Problems with Overindulgent Video Game Playing 86
   What You Can Do 87
      Know the ESRB System of Ratings 88

Chapter 6: Human Solutions 91
    Human/Relational Precautions 91
        Communication and Trust 92
        Negotiation 93
        Teaching Kids the "Rules of the Road" 94
        Online Instructional Modules 97
        Supervision 98
        Get Techno-Literate Yourself 99
        Check Your Child's Web Presence 100
        Teach Your Child to Prioritize 101
        Understand the Code: The New Shorthand 102
        Emoticons and Smileys 103
        LeetSpeak 104
        Legislation to Help Protect Children 105
        The Communications Decency Act (CDA) 106
        Child Online Protection Act (COPA) 106
        Children's Online Privacy Protection Act of 1998 (COPPA) 106
        The Children's Internet Protection Act (CIPA) 107
        Deleting Online Predators Act of 2006 (DOPA) 107
        Other Important Initiatives 108
        Internet Corporation For Assigned Names and Numbers (ICANN) 108
        Internet Crimes Against Children (ICAC) Program 109
        Project Safe Childhood (PSC) 109
        School Acceptable Use Policies (AUP) 110
        How to Advocate 110

Chapter 7: Technological Solutions 113
    Pop-Ups 113
    Blocking and Filtering Software 114
    Keylogging 116
    Other Ways to Filter/Block Sites 116
        Parental Controls on your Browser 116
        Using Your Router 116
        Child/Family Friendly Internet Service Providers 117
        Bookmarking 117
        Limited User Accounts 118
        A Few Words about Proxy Servers 118
    Computer Security 119
Summary 120
Resourceful Websites 120
Endnotes 131

Dedication

To my family who is always so supportive and encouraging. With all my heart, thank you to my wife, Betty, and sons Giuseppe and Matteo, for being you.

Preface

I appreciate you reading this book for several reasons. For one, it is a testimony to your dedication of learning more about how to better safeguard your children in a high-tech world. I don't take this for granted. Adults are busy people and today's children require, in my opinion, more time and attention than ever before. I also believe that children today are developing at a faster rate and becoming more sophisticated in how they think and in what they can do. Effective parenting and educating is more challenging as a result. I hope that this book will be the beginning of a more long term plan for your own technological literacy.

The second reason I am glad you picked up *GuardkingKids.com* is that you are important to the protection of other peoples' children, not just your own. You see, technology is ubiquitous – it's everywhere! Parents can do everything right and take all the reasonable precautions for guarding their children online and yet their child may still be vulnerable. That child need only to go visit a friends house with an Internet connected computer, cell phone, game box, or other device and be completely susceptible to high-tech trouble if the parent(s) in *that* household do not take similar precautions. By actively learning more about Internet and technology safety, you are dedicating yourself to *not* being the weakest link in a highly connected planet.

This book endeavors to achieve two primary goals. First, to increase your awareness of the types of risks that families take when allowing their children to use high-tech tools in an unsupervised and uneducated manner. There is no way that I could cover all possible risks because there are too many of them so here I will help you focus on what I believe are the most pressing. I offer some practical solutions along the way although reserve the last two chapters of the book for a comprehensive overview of methods for reducing the risk that technology poses among children. The reason for this is simply organizational. As I was writing, I realized that one solution or method for reducing high-tech risks can apply to many different problems (e.g., incorporating blocking/filtering software on your home computer). When a unique solution to a problem arises, I describe it immediately after letting you know about the issue. Also, know that when it comes to reducing the risk of high-tech trouble among kids, one size does not fit all. There are many solutions that could work for you, your family, and/or your students given your situation. Use your own judgement for what will work best for you. More often than not, you will want to use a combination of interventions. Sometimes, you can start with human solutions and then use technological solutions as if they don't work. For example, you may set up a rule in your home, no Internet after 10pm. If the children follow the rule, great. If after a while they continue to break the rule, then you can use a program that automatically shuts off the Internet connection at that time (a program called CyberSitter does a nice job of scheduling Internet access if you need it to).

GuardingKids.com

You may start to feel yourself getting upset or frustrated while reading along because you may discover that you have unwittingly allowed an unacceptable level of technological risk in your home or classroom because you were not aware. That is, with increased awareness comes potential anxiety. Quick story. When I was doing a workshop for a Parent Teacher Association one time about Technology Safety, a woman who was visibly upset stood up and began to confront me. She had given both of her children laptops without any protection such as blocking or filtering software and unlimited/unsupervised access to the Internet. She claimed that, "Kids will be kids and it's unrealistic to worry about any of this stuff!" She also said that, "If we interfere, the kids will just go underground and hide what they are doing from us." I understand that this Mom may have felt a bit uneasy knowing that she had allowed her children to be in risky situations, that is an unsettling idea. However, I told her that I disagreed with her "don't ask and don't tell" approach to kids and technology. Other people have reacted similarly and so now, at the beginning of a training, I always warn parents that they may come to realize that they made some mistakes about how they allow their children to use technology. I reassure them that we all do the best we can with what we know at any given time. And, I remind them that they are not alone – most people are not very aware of the potential risks of technology. Finally, I encourage them to embrace the idea that "It's never too late to change course." Although difficult, any decision you make with your children, with some finesse, can be changed given new information." They will not like it although remember you are not competing in a popularity contest. Indeed, they may take some actions "underground" and you cannot control that. Hopefully, however, you have developed a strong relationship which will discourage your children from doing this.

It's never too late to change course ...

Solutions for reducing risk can typically be divided into two categories – human and technological. As you will see, I highly emphasize taking human precautions such as developing a trusting and open relationship with your child, sharing the online experience, and strategically placing your Internet connected computer in a viewable area (e.g., the living room). Technological solutions such as using filters, blockers, key loggers are secondary and meant only to be a "backup" in the certain case that human error occurs. A combination of these should prove effective. However, have you noticed that I have not used the word *prevention* when it comes to safeguarding our children. As parents, we need to face the fact that, given the rapid and relentless proliferation of technology, *completely* preventing our children from possible threats is impossible. You may put into place several different safety mechanisms and yet your child may someday still, intentionally or not, view a pornographic website or talk to strangers in a chat room. As parents, we simply cannot control everything that our children do or think. The best we can do is provide an environment that is supportive and structured while teaching them the knowledge, skills, and attitudes to make responsible decisions for themselves – especially when no one else is watching. There is no such thing as a 100% guarantee.

Educational Media Corporation®, Box 21311, Minneapolis, MN 55421-0311

GuardingKids.com

As you read, try to keep a fair and balanced perspective. Technology, including the Internet, is not inherently good or evil. Albeit quite powerful, computers, cell phones, mp3 players, personal digital assistants, etc. are all tools. We judge these tools by the impact they have on us as individuals and as a society. That impact is directly related to how the person or user decides to use the tool. Every technology that I describe in these pages could easily be included in a book that showcases their usefulness and places them in a positive light. Many people will tell you that these very same technologies have made their lives easier, more interesting, and perhaps even more joyful. These technologies can bridge the distance between family members, help businesses keep a competitive edge, and automate the mundane parts of our lives so that we can focus on more meaningful activities. The Internet is not a fad but a network that will continue to become even more integrated throughout the fabric of our lives. The march of progress, for better or worse, continues unabated. How we entertain ourselves, communicate, be productive in our work – everything – will continue to change rapidly and without very good prediction.

Warning: Some things may be surprising!

There is lots of information here to digest and a great deal of it can be a bit of a surprise. After a while, you may feel like throwing your computer out the window or joining the Amish in the Pennsylvania Dutch Country. But remember, technology is not going away. We need to deal with this. We need to harness the power of technology to give our kids every advantage in competing in the global economy of the 21st century. Indeed, there are several pieces of good news. First, understanding technology and making better decisions as a result is not an event but a process. You don't have to "get it" all at once, only a little bit consistently over time. Consider technological literacy as professional development just like a lawyer who keeps up with the changing laws a little bit each week or month, you can do the same for your profession – including parenting. Second, there is a great deal of help around you. Later in the book I point out some of the many online tutorials, many of them free, to help you understand and practice. Also, you can take classes, webinars (seminars over the web), purchase videos, work with your local library, and more. I also encourage you to let your kids be the teachers and you be the student. It's a chance for them to show off their knowledge and for you both to have a shared experience.

Something else I want to point out is related to perspective. This book focuses on the potential for high-tech trouble among children and how parents, educators, and other care takers can help guard them. If you think about something half the time, you tend to believe that it happens half the time, maybe even to half the people. Realize that we are dealing with prevalent problems and issues posed by technology although the risks are certainly not pandemic. Of course, one victim of cyberbullying or sexual predation is one too many. But to believe that every child is at risk by simply logging on is not accurate. Most children use technology to interact with their real life friends and they have been smart to keep personal information private. They "get it." My recommendation is to keep your guards up and be on the defense although also put the risks into proper perspective. And, most important ... panicking, over-reacting, and being irrational won't solve any problems that may arise.

Technology is ubiquitous – its everywhere! This will take all of us!

Growing and educating responsible children is an immense challenge over the long haul. So, I've also listed some valuable resources in the form of further readings, websites, and other resources throughout the book. In addition, I've developed a website that can serve you in this endeavor well after you read the book. The address is *www.GuardingKids.com*. At this website, please share with me and others about your experiences, both pleasant and unpleasant, so that we may all learn from each other – so that as a community of care takers, we can best protect our most important natural resource – kids.

Evolution of GuardingKids.com

This book was a next step in a series of logical goals for me. My mission for the last two decades has been to help children and families succeed academically, personally, and in their careers. That is, I am interested in helping children to become responsible, productive, and likeable members of society. I've worked in the field of mental health and in schools as a school counselor. And for the last 13 years I've trained adults to become counselors in schools, the community, and in private practice as part of my duties as a university professor.

I've always been intrigued by gadgets and, at the same time, enjoyed coming up with creative solutions to every day problems. As technology rapidly evolved, I was especially captivated by its potential for helping people to achieve their goals in more effective, efficient, and enjoyable ways. The 1990's was a particularly exciting and energizing period. Technology, fueled by rapid advancements in microprocessor design as well as the development of the World Wide Web impacted every aspect of life in our country. Virtually no industry was left untouched, and no profession left unaltered by these changes. In the counseling field, practitioners explored new ways to meet and interact with clients. We saw changes in how we managed our offices and received training, consumed research, and prepared for the future. We developed new words and new concepts, and began to think about what we did in new ways because of these changes. Like most people, counselors are also awed by the ways that technology can assist us in achieving more than we could achieve without technology. We are surrounded by "smarter" machines from our automobiles that can anticipate and assist in preventing a crash to our kitchen toaster that "knows" when your pastry is hot enough. Equipment inside our homes including computers, television, stereo, and other appliances are increasingly being networked and can be operated onsite or remotely using the Internet or cellular phone. This decade witnessed the spawning of new technology related careers and made others extinct. Some of these new careers were not even envisioned 10 years ago by most Americans.[1]

As a counseling profession, we realized that learning about technology (i.e., technological literacy) was no longer just for fun, it became an issue of competency. At some point, counselors who decided to "opt out" of information technology such as the Internet found themselves to be working with students who perceived them to live in a world that no longer existed. This perception certainly does not contribute to a productive counseling relationship. Also, counselors who avoided emerging technology discovered that education, similar to business and industry, was rapidly changing and that high-tech tools were needed to keep up. Probably around the late 1990s, technological knowledge and skills became a critical component of the professional counselors' expertise in order to maintain acceptable levels of competency.

As counselors were learning about how to better leverage technology in their work, we were also noticing the potential hazards, especially among children, who are rapidly integrating technology into their lives. It has become all too clear these days that helping kids learn how to be responsible users of technology is essential. Parents, counselors, and other educators are now working to make this a standard part of technological and media literacy.

I've realized a couple of other things along the way as well. First, the risks among adults and children alike – especially children– are increasing. From social networks such as MySpace.com to instant messaging, cell phones, text messaging, exposure to pornography, bullying, hate, and inappropriate content, the level and intensity of danger is on the rise. Second, it seems to me that children are more technologically literate than their parents or guardians. This makes sense. Children are growing up in this high-tech world. They have been immersed in rapid technological developments and have grown quite accustomed to change. In contrast, their parents and other care takers grew up in a different world and have been forced to adapt. For many adults, adapting to the amazing changes brought on by technology has come with fear, avoidance, and certainly stress. This has created an imbalance between kids who are "in the know" and their parents/care takers whom are "in the dark." And because technological literacy in our current information age translates into power, kids are in some ways more powerful than their parents. This is not good. Parents are entrusted to provide appropriate structure, guidance, supervision, and much more in the course of caring for their children. Yet, a lack of understanding about technology has compromised their ability to do just that.

My attention now has turned from working with mostly professional school counselors to working more with all care takers – parents, teachers, counselors, grandparents, guardians, etc. – so that we may *all* more effectively monitor, supervise, and guard kids against high-tech trouble.

As both a professor and a parent, I thank you for learning more about this important issue. I also encourage you to share your own tips, tricks, and related recommendations with me by visiting www.GuardingKids.com.

Russell A. Sabella, Ph.D.

April, 2008

Chapter 1: Introduction

Consider the following actual excerpts from various media reports:

- A high school freshman has been suspended over the posting on MySpace.com of a 15-second video recorded in a high school classroom. It is the second time this month that high school students in Morris County were suspended over postings on MySpace.com. The video was posted on the popular social networking website by a user whose profile describes him as a 14-year-old from Flanders. The video caption explains that the clip features a substitute teacher's reaction to a student who asked whether the substitute "does coke." [2]

- The use of modern means of interpersonal and mass communication has become an essential part of being young. Technology has enabled two people to connect with each other virtually anywhere and at any time, a privilege that, according to new research, is often abused by youngsters and cutting into their sleep time. A study published in the September 2007 issue of the journal SLEEP finds that cell phone use after bedtime is very prevalent among adolescents, and its use is related to increased levels of tiredness after one year. [3]

- A high school senior who threatened the lives of at least two other students is set to face criminal charges as an adult, authorities said. Patrick, 17, was arrested after he allegedly warned a friend in MySpace.com postings and cell phone text messages to prepare for "bloodshed and a lot of people crying." Police believe the teenager intended the warning for his ex-girlfriend and her new boyfriend, who are also students at McAllen Memorial. Officers would not say Tuesday whether they had found any evidence that Patrick had intended to act upon the threat. In an e-mail message sent through MySpace.com, authorities say Patrick told his friend that he was not angry at his ex-girlfriend for leaving him, but that he wanted to get even. After the initial messages, the teen sent two text messages to his friend, saying that his ex-girlfriend and her new boyfriend were going to learn the meaning of pain, the affidavit states. [4]

- A 67-year-old man who says he doesn't even like watching movies has been sued by the film industry for copyright infringement after a grandson of his downloaded four movies on their home computer. The Motion Picture Association of America filed a federal lawsuit Tuesday against Fred Lawrence of Racine, seeking as much as $600,000 in damages for downloading four movies over the Internet file-sharing service iMesh. The suit was filed after Lawrence refused a March offer to settle the matter by paying $4,000. [5]

- A 15-year-old girl was back in Vermont Thursday, two days after going to Maine with a man she met on the Internet, police said. Ashley, of St. Albans, was found at an interstate rest area in Maine, with Chad, 18, of Rangeley. Police say the two met on the Internet. Investigators are trying to determine how long the two had been corresponding. [6]

- A suspected sexual predator made a date with a teenage girl but instead met up with the Fort Myers Police Department. Jack Rojas is the 25th man caught in an undercover sting designed to catch sexual predators. Police say Rojas insisted on meeting the undercover officer pretending to be a teenage girl. [7]

- A 17-year-old student who posted on his blog site that he was being bullied and threatened by the Plainfield School District will face an expulsion hearing this week, a local attorney said. [8]

- Nicole was just 12 years old in the summer of 2004 when she started chatting online with a 27-year-old man who called himself "Michael." The pair talked multiple times a day on the computer for weeks, until Michael thought it was time for them to meet in person. Nicole managed to keep her dangerous new "friend" a secret from her mother; it was a terrifying secret that Nicole says nearly cost her her life. Lucky for Nicole, her mother wasn't fooled long. [9]

- Franklin County authorities are investigating a text-messaging chain reaction in which high school students were passing around pornographic images by cellphone. Students at Franklin County High School were sending around pornographic images of one or more minors, said Maj. Josh Carter of the Franklin County Sheriff's Office. "It was a domino effect," Carter said, adding that at least 15 students — and possibly many more — forwarded the image. [10]

- A high school teacher was charged with sending nude pictures of herself and sex-related text messages to the cell phone of a 14-year-old student. Beth Ann Chester, a 26-year-old health and physical education teacher at Moon Area High School in suburban Pittsburgh, was charged with sexual abuse of children, statutory sexual assault and related counts. Chester sent three pictures of herself, two of them naked, to the boy's cell phone, police said. The student replied with a naked picture of himself, authorities said. [11]

- Hate groups are slowly but increasingly using the World Wide Web to appeal to women and children, according to a report by the Anti Defamation League, an organization that fights bigotry and has been monitoring the use of the Web by hate groups since 1995. The report, found that in the past two years, hate sites have added special pages aimed at broadening their influence. "It's a way to bring people into the movement," said Jordan B. Kessler, the author of the report, "Poisoning the Web: Hatred Online." Sites aimed at teen-agers, in particular "skinhead" pages featuring music with a white supremacist message, have been around for several years. Three sites found in the group's survey, however, were clearly aimed at a younger crowd, Kessler said. [12]

- San Francisco just launched the nation's first text-messaging program aimed to shoot instant cellphone messages to sexually active young people seeking advice about sex and health. The service focuses on everything from what to do "if ur condom broke" to whom to call "if ur feeling down ... like u wanna xcape ur life." [13]

GuardingKids.com

- One in five young people has been bullied by mobile phone or via the Internet, a study suggests. Children's charity NCH surveyed 770 youngsters and found 14% of 11- to 19-year-olds had been threatened or harassed using text messages. Bullies had used images taken with mobile phone cameras to intimidate or embarrass one in 10 young people. This included singling out overweight or spotty youngsters and recording and sharing acts of playground violence. The findings follow reports of so-called "happy slapping" attacks - where assaults on children and adults are recorded on mobile phones and sent via video messaging. [14]

- Hot, steamy and now downloadable: "Aural sex" shimmies into the podcast as "podnography" trend takes off. It didn't take long for sex to rear its heavy-breathing head in the world of podcasting. Now, in addition to free audio shows on music, politics and sports available for downloading onto your handy-dandy MP3 players, you can access old-fashioned — or not so old-fashioned — sexcasts as well, for repeated aural pleasure. "Is it surprising? Absolutely not. It's inevitable," says Mike McGuire, a technology analyst at GartnerG2 in San Jose. Anytime a new technology emerges, he says, sex quickly gets in on the action. Also known as "podnography," sexcasts are audio clips that anyone can record by using a computer. [15]

- Lee Waters, a high school teacher in Orlando, Fla., was the subject of an Internet offense last month. A student posted a picture of Waters on a Website and attached to it demeaning sexual comments. School officials suspended the student and Waters filed a lawsuit against the youth in an effort to make a statement about the seriousness of Internet pranks. In another case, Swissvale police brought harassment charges against a Catholic school boy who posted a phony profile on MySpace.com in which he indicated a schoolmate was homosexual. [16]

These are a few of the literally thousands of stories where kids, using the Internet to have fun and meet "friends," found themselves in more trouble than they could have imagined. According to Michael Josephson, founder of the CHARACTER COUNTS! Coalition, computers and the World Wide Web have literally changed the world by giving us access to myriad types of information, opening foreign and novel places for our perusal and letting us meet all kinds of people, almost instantly. [17] Most of the information is useful and interesting, or at least trivial and harmless. Most of the people in chat rooms are ordinary kids simply looking for a new friend or exchanging information with old ones. And, he says, that's the problem – and it's a growing one. He goes on to note that chat rooms and e-mails can be a virtual fantasyland. You can pretend to be anybody or anything you want. Unseen and anonymous, you can be "cool" in a chat room. That's awfully appealing to an awkward, isolated and "misunderstood" youth. And it's also appealing to predators looking for children to exploit: lonely children, children looking for excitement, children looking for affection, children susceptible to a fantasy.

It can happen when children are at home, in their rooms, all during the aura of silence and safety. The truth, however, is that if we are not careful, strangers can "virtually" enter our homes and groom our child to be the victim of a kidnapping, sexual assault, molestation, or other incomprehensible act. We may reduce our anxiety about the potential risks by telling ourselves that only other children are vulnerable, that it could not happen to us. Or, you might convince yourself that your child is smart enough to ward off any suspicious activity. However, Internet predators and scammers are equal opportunity victimizers who sense vulnerability and are good at making their mark. All children are susceptible no matter what their level of intelligence. They are children. Those who intend to do harm rely on "creeping complacency." They slowly massage the egos of our children, befriend them, and create a veil of trust only to violate that trust when the opportunity is right (i.e., they have minimal chance of getting caught).

GuardingKids.com

Where is the fence?

Kids see the virtual world of cyberspace as a continuation of the real world. The conversations they have in the school lunchrooms and hallways frequently continue at home in chat rooms and via cell phone messaging. This is different than how most adults see the Internet – as a separate and different world requiring different rules of engagement. As parents and caretakers, we need to treat how our children are online no different than how they behave offline. We train them to look both ways before crossing the street, not to steal things from stores, to get permission to talk to strangers. We make certain that our children use seat belts and provide them with direct supervision when in public. These types of efforts must continue and be extended into cyberspace.

In the real world, we can set up physical boundaries to help us contain our children to spaces we deem safe. When we take them to the park, we make sure our kids stay inside the fence. When we visit a video store, we stick with the children's section and we don't let them venture into the back room where the adult videos are. Schools have hallways, some have fences, and they all have procedures for making sure that kids get from one place to the other while being supervised and monitored. At home, we activate our alarm systems at night to ward off intruders. Other boundaries in the form of rules exist. We don't allow our children to play beyond a certain perimeter in our neighborhoods or communities. We wouldn't take them with us to a night club where adult activities take place. There are laws in place so that our children cannot simply go to a convenience store and purchase alcohol, tobacco, or adult magazines. If an underage child or minor takes a flight, an attendant escorts him the entire way and checks for identification when delivering the child to his destination. Technology has at least blurred if not eliminated these real world boundaries. The Internet and other high-tech gadgets has essentially introduced a high-speed interstate upon which we all travel yet a driver's license is not necessarily required. Road signs are unclear or non-existent. The small number of "rules of the road" are not typically enforced and the "strip joints" are right next door to the ice cream shops. Very few people verify a "driver's" age and traffic occurs at all hours of the day and night. The Internet connected computer in particular has become a potential "back door" for children (and others) to enter or exit our homes as they please.

The Bigger Picture

Because of the widespread media coverage, I am guessing that you are thinking mostly about social networks such as MySpace.com and the issue of sexual predators in chat rooms. For sure, these are worth our attention. Although, I also fear that these issues are overshadowing what I believe to be even more pressing issues that deserve our attention such as:

- access to pornography
- high-tech cheating and plagiarism
- cyberbullying
- distraction from academics
- addiction
- disclosing too much personal information to the world
- inappropriate content (racism, hate, pro-suicide, eating disorder)
- electronic gaming and violence

These are issues not nearly covered by the media as much, yet they interfere in our children's lives every day. *GuardkingKids.com* covers these and a number of other areas that could lead to trouble among kids in an attempt to widen the scope of your understanding. MySpace.com is a big world although only part of a much bigger world we call the Internet. That Internet is now accessed not only by computers but many other gadgets such as iPods, cellular phones, gaming devices, and handheld personal digital assistants.

GuardingKids.com

Decisions... decisions... decisions

I believe that parenting has always been a tough job although I think you would agree (even the elders I talk too agree) that it is tougher now than ever before. The world is truly getting smaller and moving faster, in large part due to technology that has bridged great divides and has afforded the power of large companies to the individual. The world is changing and its changing fast. As parents we want to help our children take advantage of these tools in a way that bests advances their development. There are more "bases" to cover in the course of supervision. There are many more options for us to consider when making decisions about how our children achieve. More now than ever before, we need to stay focused and goal oriented in a world that is chaotic and uncertain. We need to realize that "*Just because you can, doesn't mean you should.*" Just because you *can* watch 300 channels of television, doesn't mean you *should* increase the amount of time you watch television. Just because you *can* share your information with the rest of the world in the blink of an eye doesn't mean that you *should*. Just because you *can* receive a call from anywhere and at any time doesn't mean you *should* answer it.

Granted, much of technology has a high "cool factor" and can be a lot of fun. There's lots of bells and whistles out there although those bells and whistles can call unwanted attention to ourselves and can easily distract us from other more important endeavors. We have to make informed choices about the role that technology plays in our lives. One of the things I know about effective decision making is that the quality of the information is key. What you don't know *can* hurt you.

Michael Josephson who I mentioned earlier provides an eloquent and critical piece of advice for us: Like it or not, we parents have to get involved with what our kids are viewing online. We have to find out how the Web and Instant Messaging works. We have to see what websites our kids are visiting, what files they're downloading, what their Instant Messaging jargon, shorthand and slang means. We have to take control of how the Web is being used in our own homes. We have to, because we're parents, and because it's the right thing to do.

Chapter 2:
A Web of Pornography, Prejudice, and More

The Internet, from the very beginning, has been a powerful method for distributing a wide variety of information across a large number of people, and until more recently, has not been a place where particularly young children would frequent. With increased numbers of kid-friendly resources and the integration of technology in the classroom, more and more children are taking advantage of the power of the Web. Its potential for education, communication, and a sense of global community is practically limitless. However, the Internet still remains significantly an adult forum, and so it carries with it adult subjects. This raises the question: What happens when the adult themes and a child's naive explorations meet? Or worse, how may we have unwittingly allowed the World Wide Web to become a dangerous and yet unsupervised playground for our children?

Amidst the material available on the Web that is of enormous academic, career, personal, and social potential, there is also material that even the hardiest civil libertarian would probably agree is not appropriate for small children — for example, graphical depiction of child pornography, vicious racism from bigots of various stripes, and detailed instructions on how to build bombs from some highly destructive people. In some cases this material can raise questions that go beyond those of appropriateness and taste: its distribution and ownership may also be illegal, particularly within certain jurisdictions. For example, possession of child pornography is illegal as well as reprehensible. In most cases, pornography is also readily available from non-Internet related sources (your local Adult Bookstore, for example), but its availability on the Web is a particularly sensitive issue because it is harder to monitor the age of persons accessing material on the Web than to check the age of patrons at the adult bookstore. What would be your reaction if you walked into a video store and noticed that the Disney movies are mixed in with the adult videos? This is what it's like on the web.

Sex and pornography occur in every part of the Internet. This includes the World Wide Web, Virtual Communities, online simulation games, chatrooms, instant messaging, photo sharing sites, social networks, and newsgroups to name a few. The presentation of sexually explicit materials differs from platform to platform, as does the degree of obscenity or indecency. While some are more visible than others, sexually explicit material can be easily found on all of them. Put simply, pornography is where you find it. In November, 2004, Senator Sam Brownback (R-Kansas), chair of the *Senate Commerce Committee's Science, Technology and Space Subcommittee*, described a hearing about the addictive characteristics of online pornography the most disturbing one he'd ever seen in the Senate. Brownback said porn was ubiquitous now, compared to when he was growing up and "some guy would sneak a magazine in somewhere and show some of us, but you had to find him at the right time."

The nature of the Web itself — a multimedia carnival of pictures, movies, sounds, and colors — makes it much more popular with the general public than the other platforms. The multimedia aspect of the Web also makes it a place where all kinds of sexual material can be displayed, and many people, including children, have taken advantage of this both for profit and for fun. This is especially true with the evolution of Web 2.0 – a web developed by you and me. In the Web 2.0 world, companies provide the "microphone" and we do the "talking." In fact, you may recall that Time Magazine's Person of the Year in 2006 was You. Lev Grossman of Time Magazine wrote, "The new Web is a very different thing. It's a tool for bringing together the small contributions of millions of people and making them matter. " Unfortunately, many of those so called contributions are, although legal, not very appropriate for children.

This chapter endeavors to make you more aware of how some children may easily access "XXX" rated material. In addition, I'll overview how the Web is sometimes used to promote some very destructive ideas/activities such as racism, eating disorders, self-injury, and suicide.

Accidental Exposure: Pornography Plays Dirty

Most pornographers seem to be tricky and clever people. They have thought through how to increase the likelihood that, when people are searching for legitimate sites, that they accidentally land on their own adult themed websites. Although the following example is no longer true, it is a classic example of what I mean. For years, when children, teachers, and others wanted to take advantage of the information-rich website of the White House, they would accidentally navigate to the wrong website, http://www.whitehouse.com instead of http://www.whitehouse.gov. This is understandable, an easy mistake to make, because most websites on the Internet end in .com. For a long time, http://www.whitehouse.com was a pornographic site.

The good news is that the PROTECT Act created a new federal law that makes it a crime to knowingly use a misleading domain name on the Internet with the intent to deceive a minor into viewing material that is harmful to minors on the Internet. The provision, copied from an older stand-alone bill called the Truth in Domain Names Act, makes it a crime to "knowingly use a misleading domain name on the Internet with the intent to deceive a person into viewing material constituting obscenity." This crime carries a penalty of up to four years in prison and/or a fine. An offender might commit this crime, for example, by using a domain name that features the name of a popular children's cartoon character, purposefully misspelled, and leads to a website featuring harmful materials harmful. The new law also makes it a crime to use a misleading domain name on the Internet with the intent to deceive any person into viewing obscenity, which carries a penalty of up to two years imprisonment and/or a fine.

The Department of Justice continues to prosecute violators of the Truth In Domain Names provisions of the PROTECT Act.[18] For example, in February 2004, one man was sentenced by a federal judge in Manhattan to 30 months in prison on charges that he created and used misleading domain names on the Internet to deceive minors into logging on to pornographic websites. Those domain names included close misspelling of domains names that are popular with children, such as "www.dinseyland.com," (a variation on Disney Land's website) and "www.bobthebiulder.com," and "www.teltubbies.com" (variations on the websites for "Bob the Builder" and "Teletubbies"). This man allegedly owned more than 5,500 such domains, and if you happened to land on one, your visit was almost certainly unpleasant. The pornographer blitzed visitors with advertising for adult websites. Closing one browser window would cause three more to pop up, until the only escape for many web users is to force their browser, or even their whole computer, to shut down. The man is widely reported to have made millions of dollars from such web traffic.

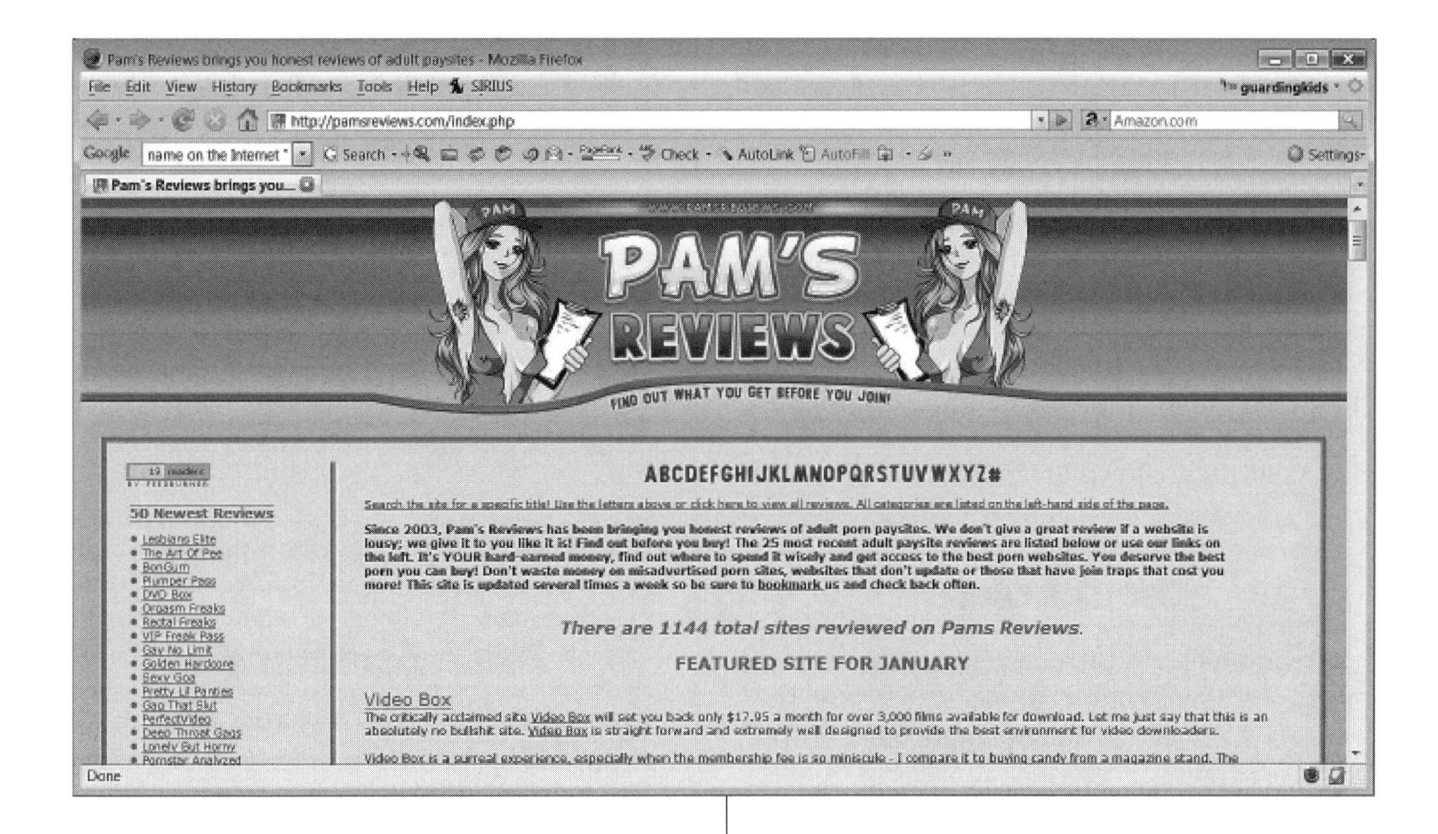

The Truth in Domain Act seems to be helping although we shouldn't let our guard down just yet. Pornographers have found other ways to accomplish the same goal (i.e., luring children and others to their adult themes sites) by using domain names that are unsuspecting. For example, http://www.hairywebsites.com/ does not contain the word "porn" or clearly allude to anyone's anatomical body parts yet it is a porn site. As is typical, this site also makes it easy to visit other porn sites and even gives reference to a toll free number to "talk live with really hairy women." Similarly, http://pamsreviews.com/ is a review site for "the best in adult paysites" yet you wouldn't know this by the domain name. What I find especially abhorrent about this site, and I suspect that it's not the only one, is that if you stumble on this site and decide not to enter by clicking on Exit, you are directed to another website, http://www.f9k.com/, which contains a multitude of pornographic links and content!

Yet another method for getting users (including children) to unintentionally land on pornographic websites is the practice of redirecting. Here's how it works: When someone or some organization registers their domain name (the name that you type in your web browser to navigate to a certain website), they purchase the rights or ownership to that name for a certain time. That is, the domain name registration eventually expires. If the owner fails to renew for whatever reason, the domain name is "up for grabs" by anyone else who wants to own it. This feature of the management of the domain name system is thought to be desirable since it allows and facilitates a turnover of names from those uninterested in using them to those who in fact do seek to put them to active use. But this structure also allows domains to be renewed by firms who do not seem to seek to use the domains to offer original content but rather seem to hope to profit from the prior promotional works of others. In one case study, a Harvard Law School graduate candidate found 4,525 distinct domains that all redirect to the page entitled "Tina's Free Live Webcam (which, quite ironically, was bought by another company)."[19]

GuardingKids.com

Of course, purchasing the domain of a former website frequently used by children is the part that I'm worried about most. For example, The Black Diamond Girl Scouts had http://www.blackdiamondgirlscouts.com registered to them and they used it for their Girl Scout site. They decided that the domain name was too long, so they bought a new one and gave up the old one (they are now http://www.bdgsc.org/). Within a short time span, the domain was bought and used to re-direct traffic to pornography (once again, thank goodness, it was bought and is now used for a non-pornographic site).

Direct Access

I won't mention them here lest I advertise for them more than is necessary for helping you, but there are a ton of pornographic websites out there that are only a few clicks away. A child need only discover these, probably from their classmates, and type in the address in any web browser. Once landing on hard-core adult sites, children can view photos, watch movies, and click on links to visit one of hundreds of thousands of other porn sites. Many of the very graphic XXX sites do not verify a user's age whatsoever. They simply warn the visitor of impending adult material which, as you know, for an adolescent serves as further enticement. Other sites do not even spare the viewer and present the adult material right on the home page.

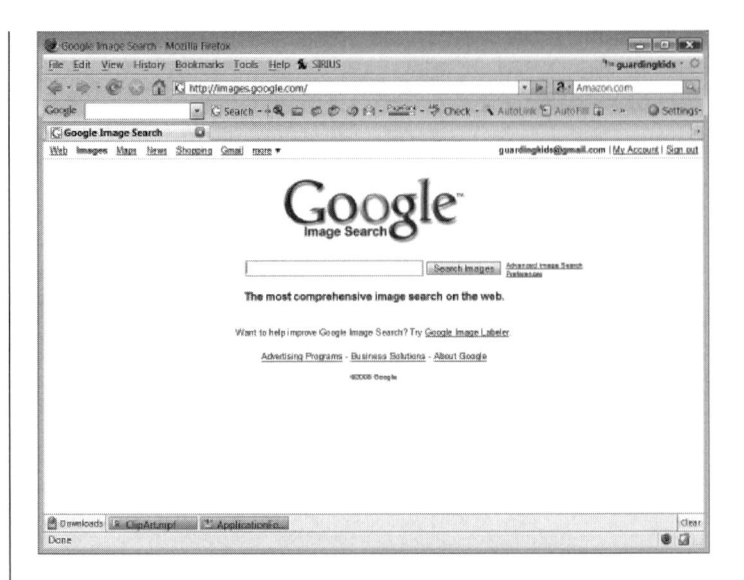

Basic Searching

"If I can operate Google, I can find anything... Google, combined with Wi-Fi, is a little bit like God. God is wireless, God is everywhere and God sees and knows everything. Throughout history, people connected to God without wires. Now, for many questions in the world, you ask Google, and increasingly, you can do it without wires, too."

Alan Cohen, V.P. of Airespace, a new Wi-Fi provider, New York Times, 6/29/03

Indeed, with just the right key words, powerful search engines like Google.com, Yahoo.com, MSN.com, and Altavista.com, can help anyone find inappropriate material in just a second or two. And because our children are learning more sexually charged and risqué language at an earlier age, it becomes increasingly probable that they might one day decide to put one of those words in the same search engine that they've been using as part of a classroom project. As of this writing, the keyword "shit" produces over 177 million results. Not all of these will lead to pornographic material, however they are all websites that would probably be at least inappropriate. In some cases, the website's title may use childish humor and be especially attractive to our youth. For instance, one site describes its purpose as the following:

GuardingKids.com

"The Shit list is a mailing list where four people from around the country (learn about them on our bio page) post a message every time they take a shit, and everyone who subscribes to this list gets to hear about it. Their posts range from a quick description of the feces to an in-depth musing of the effects of a good dump on the American work ethic. Anyhow, it's funny shit."

Kids are curious and clever. Given the chance, they will at one time or another type in the keyword "sex" or worse, something like "pussy." As you might imagine, included on the top of the results page are sites which would probably make the likes of Larry Flynt (founder of Hustler magazine) blush.

Unfortunately, the search words that our children may use don't even have to be that graphic. Put the words "papa smurf" in any search engine and you'll get links to pages such as "*Papa Smurf Can I Lick Your Butt?*" and "*The Sexual Adventures of the Smurfs.*" Clicking on one of the first links on the results page reveals a short animated movie depicting these cartoon characters singing an X-rated song performing anilingus and smoking drugs.

No matter what the search engine, the key to accessing pornography is turning off the search engine's family filter. What may shock you is just how easy it is to turn filtering off. I conducted a search on six major search engines (Google, AOL, MSN, Altavista, Yahoo!, and Dogpile) using the keyword *pussy* to see what would happen and what the degree of difficulty would be for actually accessing adult material. All six of the search sites had, by default, at least a moderate level of filtering turned on and alerted me to the fact that I may be accessing adult material. The alerts also included the fact that "filtering" was in place and conveniently provided a link to changing this preference. All six search sites allowed me to turn the filter off within five (5) clicks of the mouse, and all without any age verification. To be fair, Yahoo! was the only one of these search sites that allowed me to password protect the filter setting although this could be turned off by any Yahoo! user who is registered and who reported to be 18 years or older. However, even with Yahoo!'s search filter on, I was able to view two sites that were pornographic in nature. That is, the filter did not completely work. The same exact situation was true for Altavista. America Online did allow me to turn on a condition that future searches would be limited to only inside AOL's network. This seemed to help although, again, was not 100% safe.

Basic Image Searches

In addition to searching websites using basic key words, any user can essentially bring pornographic images garnered from the millions of websites into one convenient place. All the popular search engines now have the capability of searching for only images. Try it yourself. Go to http://images.google.com and enter simple keywords such as "vagina," "cock," "breast," or "suck" to name a few and the results are astounding. Hundreds of thousands of images, which can be filtered by size or color, are ready for viewing. Again, the trick with all of the popular search engines is that the built in filters must first be turned off which literally requires only four to five clicks. Also know that because most of the resulting images reside on pornographic websites, this opens the gate to other images, videos, and yet more links to other XXX-rated sites. Realize too that there exists free software that allows anyone to bypass the time consuming viewing and downloading of graphics by just typing in a keyword and downloading hundreds of graphics per minute right to one's own computer.

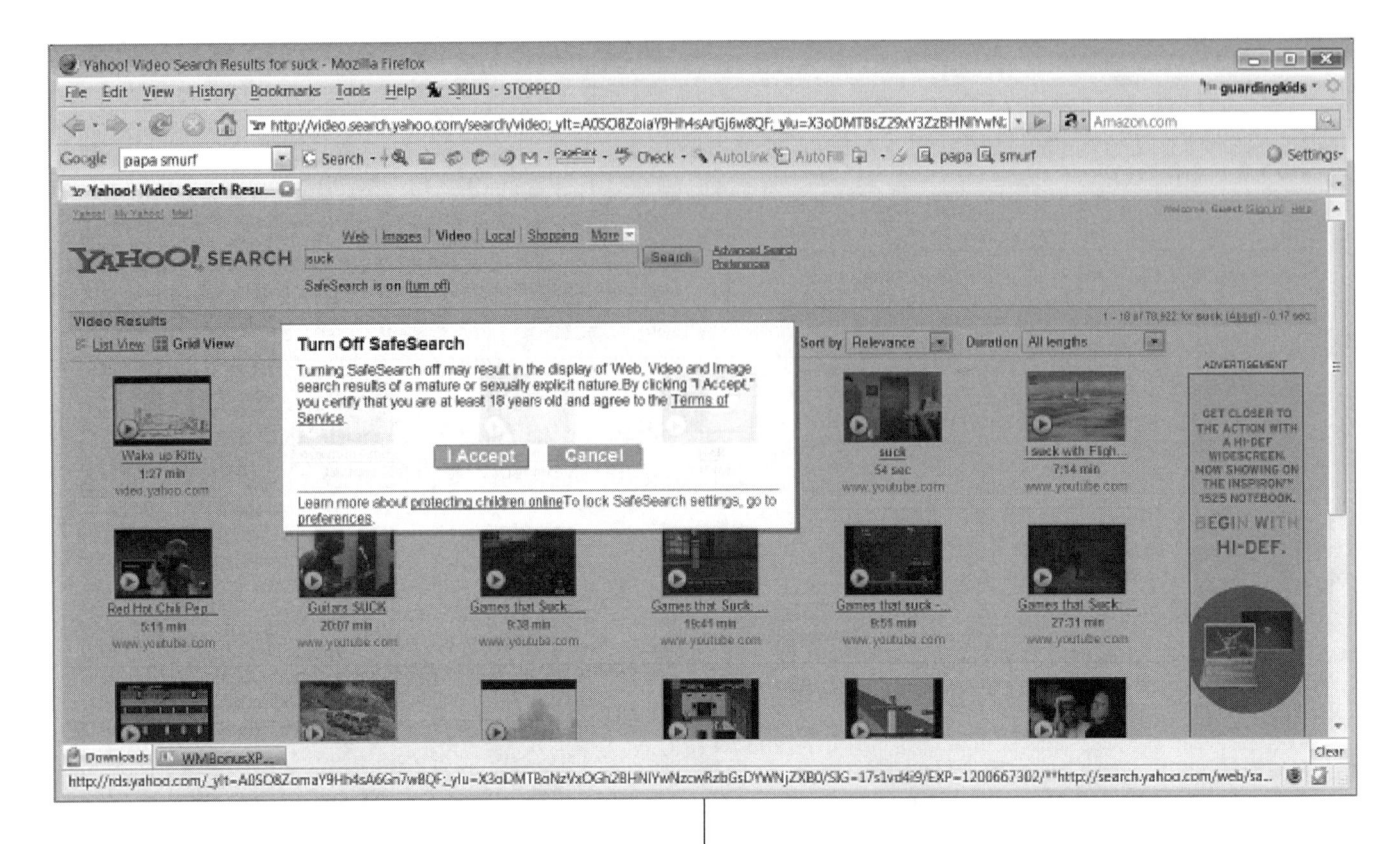

Basic Video Searches

Add the words "free video" to other pornographic keywords and any child is likely to gain access to sample XXX-rated videos – samples of what they could get if they became a member of the pornography service. Similar to searching for images, all the major search engines can now search for video and filter them by length, title, website domain, and format. In fact both Yahoo! and Google continue to become more sophisticated by analyzing the text around video links on the Web and the data embedded in video to index the content (Google can even capture the text from the closed captioning of each program/video as it airs). Both Yahoo! and Google both allow anyone to also upload video where users will be able to search, preview, purchase and play it. As of this writing, Google.com does not seem to include pornography although Yahoo! Video (http://video.yahoo.com/) and AltaVista video search (http://www.altavista.com/video/) both do.

You don't need to go to a major search engine to quickly find inappropriate videos. Some sites specialize in allowing people to share (upload and download) and search for videos. These sites (I'll mention a few examples in just a bit) contain mostly silly videos although are scattered with inappropriate content. When you click to watch a video with a provocative title, you receive the following message: *This video may contain content that is inappropriate for some users, as flagged by [site name] user community. To view this video, please verify you are 18 or older by logging in or signing up.* The **only** age verification is first inputting your birth date and then agreeing to a statement, "- I certify I am over 13 years old." That's it. Once signed up as an adult (whether the user is really an adult or not), the user gets the following message when clicking on adult content: *By clicking "Confirm," you are agreeing that all videos flagged by the [site name] community will be viewable by this account.* Many video sharing sites exist all over the web including some of these popular ones:

- *http://video.google.com*
- *http://www.ifilm.com/*
- *http://photobucket.com/*
- *http://video.yahoo.com/*
- *http://www.pornotube.com*
- *http://www.dailymotion.com/*
- *http://www.vsocial.com/*
- *http://www.youtube.com*
- *http://www.vimeo.com/*
- *http://www.putfile.com/*
- *http://www.veoh.com/*

Advanced Web Searching

Some children with advanced searching skills may use techniques that go beyond doing the previously described basic searches. By using advanced knowledge and techniques, they may also figure out ways to get around filters and other blocks. Two common work-arounds are to search by file type and directories.

File Type

Any popular search engine also allows the user to limit their results by file type. So, for instance, one can type in as the keyword the name of any well-known porn star and limit the results to a popular multimedia formats such as Microsoft PowerPoint. Files such as PowerPoint are especially good at delivering images and even video to anyone that wants them. And, if the PowerPoint is limited to only graphics, a powerful search engine such as Google may not be able to correctly identify (i.e., index) the file as possibly adult rated. Try this: Go to Google.com and type in [jenna jameson filetype:ppt] (without the brackets) and you'll notice a list of links which point to only PowerPoint files (e.g., http://tinyurl.com/2w9wqe or http://tinyurl.com/2kc2uh) which can be either viewed online or downloaded for easy viewing on one's computer at any time and in any place. Our children don't even have to know search conditions such as filetype:ppt because search engines allow the user to filter by file type simply by pointing and clicking, normally choosing the file type from a drop down menu. This particular feature of each search engine is usually found under the Advanced Search menu. In fact, a user can also filter out an entire domain such as educational institutions so that they do not waste their time finding results that are more academic in nature such as reports, papers, and research. So, for example, the following search in Google.com will result in only PowerPoint files that are found on commercial websites thus increasing the chances of finding exactly what you want: "jenna jameson" filetype:ppt site:com

Directories

Sometimes people collect adult material (as well as illegal music, games, and more) and store it in folders on their own websites so they can access the files from anywhere they are and share them with others. Other folks have figured out that they can use search engines to locate these folders which frequently results in a jackpot of files. The reason that a folder or directory of files sometimes shows up instead of a web page is because the folder lacks a special type of file called an index or default page. Unless you otherwise specify a particular web page, your web browser will automatically look for the index or default page. For example, when you visit Google.com, you are actually accessing http://www.google.com/index.html. In the absence of these default files, and if the folder has not been protected by the web designer, a directory of files will show up.

The trick to finding these directories is guessing what the web designer named the folder and knowing a simple search term to find it. The search phrase is "index of \name" where the word name can be the name of any folder. To search for folders on the web that are named Jenna, you would type: "index of \jenna" (this time include the quotes so that the search engine searches for these words as an intact phrase). Then all one has to do is to click on each file to hear it, see it, or experience it. Again, the user needs only to save the files on another gadget or portable device to access these files at any time or in any place. This little trick is so popular that a website now exists that makes it quite easy. G2P (Google to Person at http://www.g2p.org) uses some crafty Google searches to help locate open directories or otherwise shared files. It is much easier to remember http://g2p.org than the complex search strings needed to delve deep into website directories.

Unsolicited E-mails

You and I affectionately know them as spam – the unrequested, unsolicited e-mails in our Inbox that, without failure, arrive on a daily basis. They tease (or annoy) us with cryptic and nonsensical subjects such *As seen on CBS News! Toronto Pharmacy Drugs qgf qi, Buy Hydrocodone online, 1 day sale, Degree award: Re-nomination, Stunning Rolex and LV replicas online, and Keep her happy with Viagra*. Now and then, the spam is so silly that it doesn't even makes sense. It looks like a bunch of random words, many of which are misspelled. Some e-mail spam, as you certainly know, is not so cryptic – to the point and quite sexual in nature.

You are probably left to wonder, "How could I have been included on an e-mail list that would be used for such offensive purposes?" "Why am I getting this stuff?" Or worse, "How did this end up in my child's e-mail account?"

How *did* you get on the spammer's list? I answer this question in much more detail in Chapter 4 although I'll address it briefly here. This could have happened in a variety of ways. First, you may have your e-mail address listed on a web page or news group out there somewhere letting others know how they can e-mail you. Spammers use programs that harvest as many e-mails as possible into a database that they use to achieve their deeds. Most of the time, the harvesting programs look for nothing but an e-mail address, other times, the programs look for e-mail addresses surrounded by certain keywords so that their resulting lists are more focused. This is important for the sale of such lists to marketers and leads us to the second way that your e-mail address ended up in someone's database – it was sold to others. Getting on one list means that you will probably be on many other lists, even when you remove the e-mail address from the web page.

Another way that you are included in spam lists is by entering this information on a web page that requires it for a sweepstakes, drawing, or perhaps in exchange for a "free" download. You don't even have to do this on a website. If you give your e-mail address to others for similar reasons (do you remember that survey you completed at the mall?), you may end up receiving unsolicited e-mails.

Web Enabled Gadgets

Just because a child (or adult for that matter) is not sitting in front of the computer does not mean that they are not accessing adult material. The web is truly becoming ubiquitous and can be accessed via cell phones, gadgets such as PlayStation Portables, and handheld computers. Think about all the electronics that your child may have access to and find out if they are "web-enabled." Remember that these gadgets can access the web wirelessly and so where there is a signal there is a way. That signal can come from your home wireless network, outside an office building, in a school, at the local Internet café, and even whole communities. Wireless routers are becoming increasingly powerful and reaching out greater distances. So, even if you don't have wireless access in your home, your neighbor may unwittingly be supplying your child with a gateway to the rest of the world.

GuardingKids.com

Web Enabled Gadgets

Other Inappropriate Websites

I think we all know that content on the World Wide Web meets with very little censorship. In the United States and some other countries, no other communication medium compares to the Internet for how rigorously people have exercised their right to freedom of speech. However, I'm not sure you appreciate the extent to which this is true. Visiting a few websites to see for yourself will show you what I mean ...

Racism, Prejudice and Hate

These are samples of websites that promote hate, prejudice, and racism:

- http://www.aryan-nations.org/
- http://www.tightrope.cc/jokes.htm
- http://www.godhatesfags.com/
- http://www.kkk.bz/
- http://www.zundelsite.org/english/harwood/Didsix01.html
- http://www.stormfront.org/forum/
- http://www.freeyourmindproductions.com/
- http://www.resist.com/
- http://www.bcpl.net/~rfrankli/hatedir.pdf

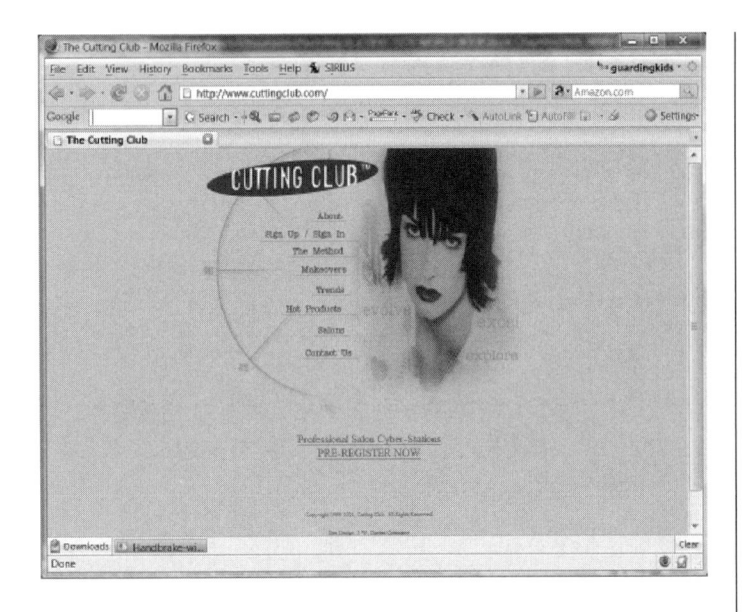

Self-Injury

These are samples of websites that promote "cutting" or self-injury, especially among girls:

- http://www.cuttingclub.com/
- http://community.livejournal.com/razor_dreams/
- http://community.livejournal.com/icut/
- http://allphilosophy.com/topic/show/344
- http://www.palace.net/~llama/psych/injury.html

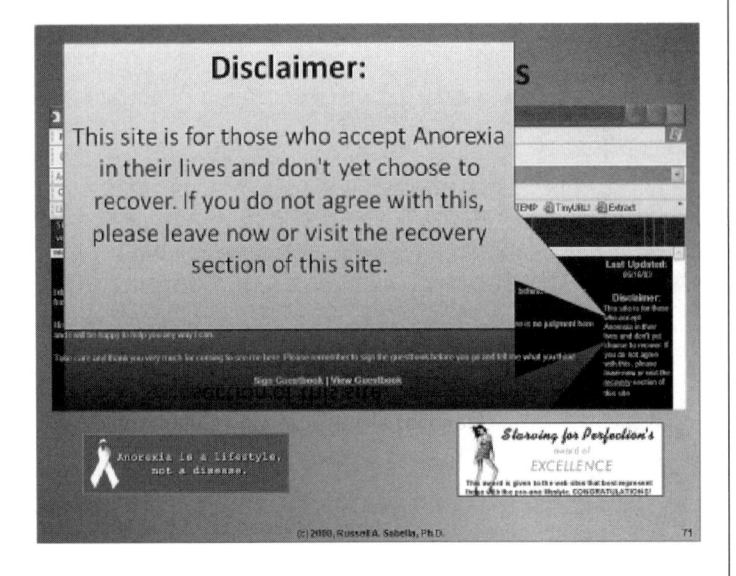

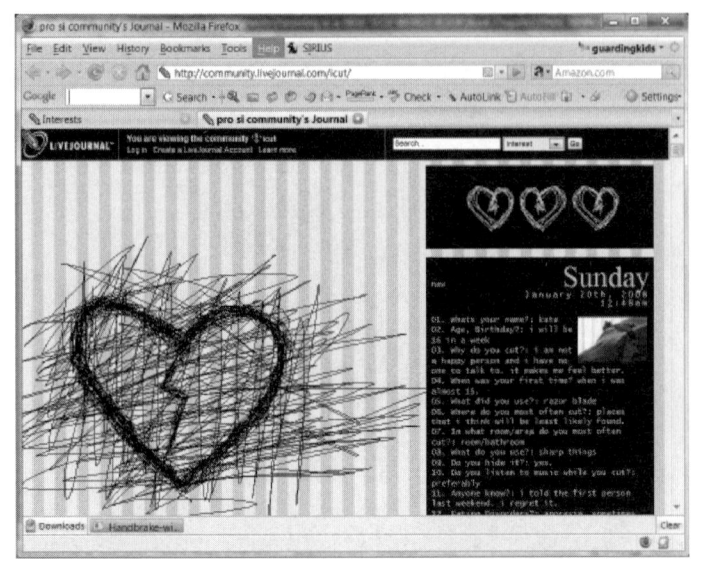

Eating Disorders

These websites, very few of many, promote eating disorders, especially anorexia nervosa and/or bulimia (also known as "pro ana" sites) as a lifestyle choice, not a disorder. Many sites are created as clubs or online support groups where those with eating disorders help each other persist in this issue:

- http://grotto.projectshapeshift.net/
- http://www.youtube.com/watch?v=hplN3IEuuo4
- http://www.proanamia.com/
- http://community.livejournal.com/proanorexia
- http://www.houseofthin.com/
- http://board.ringsworld.com/pro~ana.html

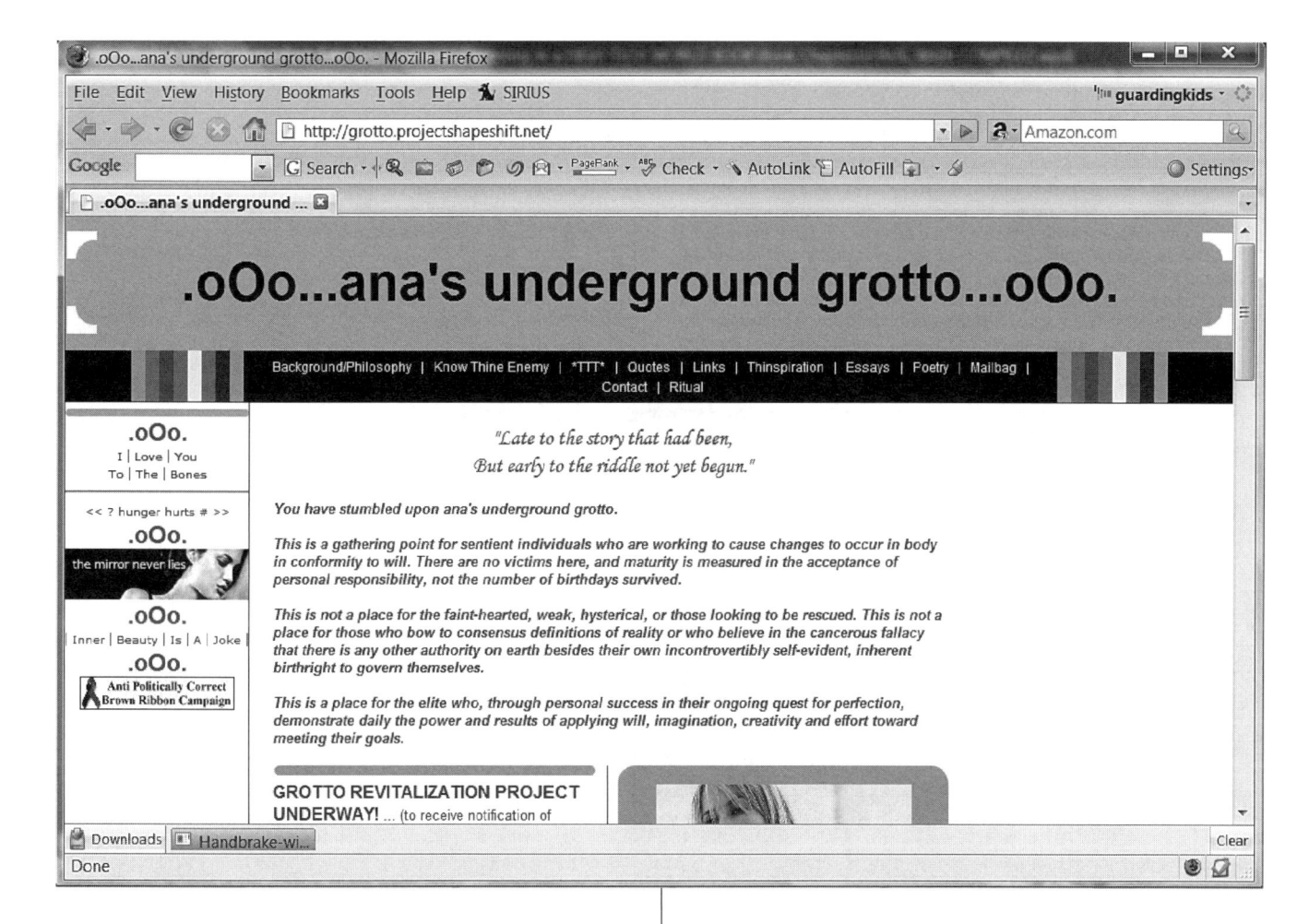

Suicide

Here is a sample of pro-suicide sites. [20] These sites range from poking fun, to providing encouragement, to giving detailed methods for killing oneself:

- http://ashbusstop.org/
- http://www.dmoz.org/Society/Death/Suicide/Methods/
- http://listverse.com/health/top-10-ways-to-commit-suicide/
- http://tinyurl.com/2k8966
- http://www.mouchette.org/suicide/answers.php3?cat=experience
- http://www.noob.us/entertainment/how-to-commit-suicide-like-a-real-man

GuardingKids.com

Chapter 3: High Tech Piracy

At one point or another, all kids will steal, cheat, or misrepresent themselves to get what they want. Generally speaking, it's a normal part of appropriate child development in which case the child tests their boundaries. Nonetheless, it's up to you as a parent or caretaker to help them learn the importance of honesty and working diligently to earn stuff, including good grades. Taking a candy bar out of the store without paying for it, copying answers from a classmate, downloading software hacks, or allowing a classmate to write a paper for you – all of these can turn into important opportunities for learning throughout childhood. We need to help kids understand the rules and the consequences of ill gotten gain. Guarding children against high-tech theft helps them to develop character and moral fortitude. As important is how we can help kids guard against the consequences of these actions which can have a lifelong impact.

As you might imagine, technology is making the situation just a bit more complicated. Even adults are sometimes confused about exactly what constitutes piracy or when someone's intellectual property rights have been violated. Yet, we need to understand the issue to better educate our children about this high-tech risk.[21] Children and adults are getting into serious trouble from committing all types of theft. Check out these headlines:

- **Florida Man Gets Six Years in Prison For Software Privacy.** The owner of a major software piracy Website was sentenced to six years in prison yesterday, one of the longest jail terms ever imposed for the growing crime of stealing copyrighted computer products, prosecutors said. U.S. District Judge T.S. Ellis III in Alexandria also ordered Danny, 37, to pay restitution of more than $4.1 million and to forfeit a wide variety of luxury goods he bought with millions of dollars in proceeds. [22]

- **Students punished for using computers inappropriately.** More than 200 midstate students were punished last school year for something other than fighting or cheating. Students were sent to detention or Saturday school for computer-related violations ranging from downloading music and altering online teacher assignments to viewing pornography, gambling or playing other games on school computers. [23]

- **Language exams faked.** Eleven graduates of the Miklós Zrinyi National Defence College were refused their degrees pending an investigation into whether they had submitted fake language certificates. But, as one student wrote on an online forum: "Other types of cheating are outdated, now you pay somebody to take the exam for you." Online classifieds site http://apronet.hu/ turns up around 20 ads offering "to sort out an official language exam for you that's good for everything." "What could look better on your shelf than a language exam!:) If you need it, we'll arrange it," reads another example. [24]

- **Norwegian Student Ordered to Pay for Hyperlinks to Music.** Norway's Supreme Court ruled Thursday that a student whose Napster.no homepage (no relation to the U.S. Napster, apparently) had links to free Internet music files must compensate the music industry. The around 170 links to mp3s will cost its creator $15,900. In a summary of its ruling, the supreme court said the music was clearly published in violation of copyright law. [25]

- **You've got lawsuit: Father sued for teen's downloads.** Dave B. was shocked when he learned last month that he was being sued by the recording industry for the downloading of hundreds of songs, including "All You Wanted" by Michelle Branch, "Eat You Alive" by Limp Bizkit and "U Don't Have to Call" by Usher. Dave, 48, a motorcycle salesman from Racine, listens to nothing but Led Zeppelin and The Doors and can barely turn on the computer. "I don't have anything with Usher or anything like that," he said. "And I've never downloaded music in my life. I thought it was a joke." It's not. Two years ago, Dave's teenage daughter downloaded more than 600 songs on their home computer through Kazaa, Internet software that allows users to swap music for free. [26]

- **Espionage on campus** is turning Joe College into James Bond as students try literally to steal better grades. The cutting-edge tools at their disposal include tiny spy cameras, noticeable only on extremely close inspection, hidden in beepers, watches and baseball caps. Florida private eye Gregg Colton has seen it all. He chases such cheats for a living, exposing cameras hidden in jackets, on ties and in purses. "These cameras are easily worn by anyone wanting to walk into a room. And they are capable of either direct recording onto a VCR, or transmission outside of the building to a waiting car," says Colton. [27]

- **High-tech Cheating Leads to Injuries.** With nearly four students vying for every available spot in China's universities, cheating on entrance exams is rampant. As technology has entered the equation for cheaters, so has it become a tool for proctors trying to defeat the cheaters. Video cameras and cell-phone blocking have become common in Chinese testing centers. Students intent on cheating resort to ever-smaller devices, with some students finding out how small is too small. According to the "China Daily," one student used an earpiece for cheating that was so tiny it entered his ear canal and ruptured his eardrum. Another student had to have an earpiece removed surgically, according to the paper, and yet another was injured when a remote listening device exploded. The device was strapped to the student's body and connected to headphones; the explosion left the student with an open wound in his abdomen. [28]

So *exactly* how are kids at high tech risk for theft? In the remainder of this chapter, I'll let you know about several common practices that could get them (and you) into trouble. These include downloading or copying media, sharing or making available to others copyrighted media/software, cheating, plagiarizing, and "cracking" software.

GuardingKids.com

Downloading Music, Movies, and More

Here are what some kids are saying about downloading and copying music/movies:[29]

IT shouldn't be illegal," said 14-year-old Sonya. "It's not like I'm selling it."

"Isn't it like recording television movies?" asked Korbi, 13. "They're making a big thing out of nothing."

"It's wrong to be downloading hundreds of songs, but if you only want one or two, it's not that big a deal," said 13-year-old Kristina.

"Individual musicians are not necessarily suffering, either," one student said. "They're not losing money, because we still buy the T-shirts and go to their concerts. They're still famous."

"The record industry is simply greedy. The industry should not be going after a bunch of kids. And how are we supposed to afford the high cost of CD's?"

"Why do they sell PC's with CD burners if it's illegal?"

Most adults understand that no matter how much money a company makes, taking something without paying for it is stealing nonetheless. It doesn't matter that what a child takes from Walmart only costs $1.29, it's still stealing. And, further, it is not a victimless crime. Other consumers must make up for the loss of profit which means that the rest of us pay more for other merchandise and security measures as a result. In a high-tech world, a child (or anyone else for that matter) need not hide the merchandise they want to steal, nor do they have to sneak it out of a store. They don't have to worry too much about store employees or cameras that could catch them in the action. Today, stealing can take only seconds and can be done in the comfort of one's own home. The chances of "getting busted" are minimal and, in fact, many kids don't even perceive high-tech theft as stealing at all. Theirs seems to be a downloading culture. A few clicks of a mouse bring them not just music, but movies, games, and hundreds of dollars of software as well. Legality seems to be a fleeting thought as they click their way through licensing agreements, impatient for the software or files at the other end.

How do kids find and download stuff for free? Sometimes its as easy as a kid who copies a song from a CD (called ripping) and e-mails the resulting MP3 file to their friends as attachments. Friend saves the attachment and again adds another song to their expansive collection. Some kids are "zipping" whole albums into one file which can then easily be sent to others, especially given that e-mail services now allow very large files to be transferred and stored, for free. If a file is too large, they can always use one of many free online services that allows a user to upload a large file and e-mail a link to that file to several others for download. Such services includes http://www.gigasize.com/, http://www.yousendit.com/, http://www.sendthisfile.com/, http://www.transferbigfiles.com/, http://megaupload.com, and http://rapidshare.de to name a few. As previously mentioned, other times people are actually ripping their songs and other media files and putting them up on the web so that they can access the songs from anywhere in the world (or intentionally share them with others).

A third way that kids find and download music is by simply visiting websites that provide links to known music files such as http://www.airmp3.net/ or http://free-music-downloads.ws/. You are probably wondering how websites like this can continue to exist without being sued. I'm not a lawyer, although from my understanding, they can do this because they are not storing any of the illegal files on their equipment. Instead, they are merely finding links to music stored by others and indexing those links for easy access and retrieval. In essence, they are just pointing the way to the culprits. Kids also get access to music files via chat rooms and instant messaging programs which now have the capability for transferring files . Other kids are burning CD's from their collections of legally downloaded music and handing it over to others. Software does also exist to quickly "backup" the thousands of songs on the iPods of some children and transfer them to another computer. Similarly, software exists on the web to make copies of protected DVD movies.

Peer-to-Peer (P2P) File Sharing

According to the Federal Trade Commission (FTC), every day, millions of computer users share files online. Whether it is music, games, or software, file-sharing can give people access to a wealth of information. And they are doing it using Peer-to-Peer (P2P) networks. You simply download special software that connects your computer to an informal network of other computers running the same software. Millions of users could be connected to each other through this software at one time. The software often is free and easily accessible and includes such popular ones as:

- Kazaa (http://www.kazaa.com/)
- Limewire (http://www.limewire.com/)
- BitTorrent (http://www.bittorrent.com/)
- Shareaza (http://www.shareaza.com/)
- Morpheus (http://morpheus.com/)

To be more specific, P2P software has each user put in a special folder any and all files that they want to share: movies, music, software, photos ... whatever. By placing the files in the designated folder, they are essentially allowing others to find, access and download the file using the users own computing resources (i.e., bandwidth and computing power). What makes this type of file sharing so powerful is that the files are indexed and searchable for very rapid identification. Also, if the P2P system detects an identical file on someone else's computer, it will actually determine the fastest way to download it. Given today's powerful computers and fast bandwidth, it doesn't take very long to download very large files, including movies.

From talking with kids and those who use P2P, my guess is that movies, pornography, and software serial numbers are the most popular files being shared.

File sharing in general and P2P sharing in particular comes with a number of risks. For example:

- When you are connected to file-sharing programs, you may unknowingly allow others to copy private files you never intended to share;
- You may download material that is protected by the copyright laws and find yourself bogged down in legal issues;
- You could easily download a virus or be part of a security breach;
- Also, it is somewhat well known that P2P software tends to interfere with other programs on your computer;
- Finally, a very common risk is that you may unwittingly download pornography labeled as something else.

I can't think of anything that you can get from being part of a P2P that is worth any one of these risks. My recommendation is to simply not use public P2P applications that are not specifically designed for productivity in the workplace.

If you have P2P software installed and you want to remove it, realize that in some instances closing an existing file-sharing program window does not actually close your connection to the network. Even when you exit the program, file-sharing may continue in the background and could increase your security risk. You must completely uninstall the software. For example visit http://www.pchell.com/support/kazaa.shtml to learn how to completely uninstall Kazaa and the programs that it comes bundled with. Use a search engine with the words "remove" (no quotes) and the name your P2P program to get the details for getting it off your computer.

So what else should I know about downloading music?

For a list of frequently asked questions and answers about copyrighted music and downloading, visit http://www.campusdownloading.com

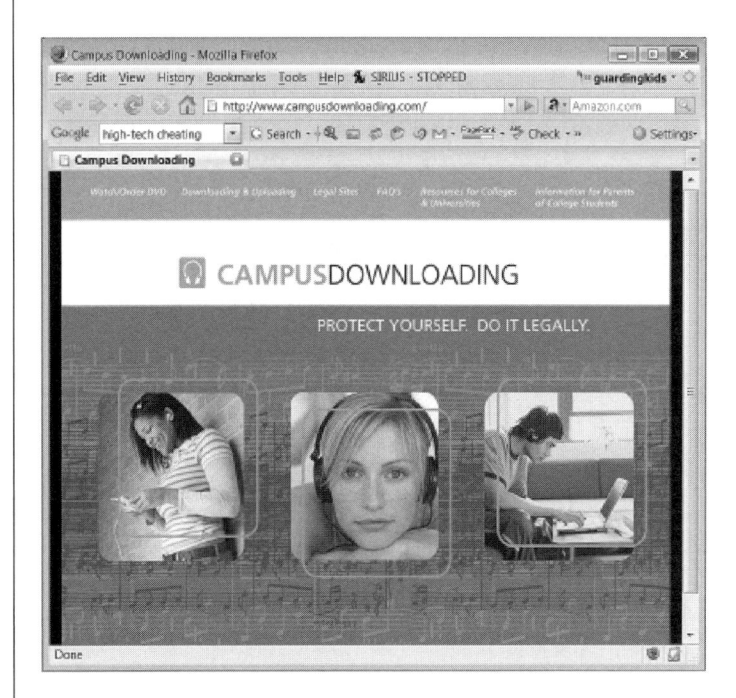

Cheating

Do you remember how you may have cheated in school? Let's see if I can guess... you wrote the answers on a out-of-view part of your body like your ankle or palm; you put together a "cheat sheet" that you could pull in and out of your sleeve; or maybe you passed notes or looked onto someone else's work to get the answer you were looking for. Like just about everything else, cheating has also gone high-tech. As a middle school counselor in the 1990's, I remember my first glimpse of this when kids would bring pagers to school. Others students could page them with numbers corresponding to the test questions and answers. Looking back, that seems archaic now as compared to cheating techniques that take advantage of more capable and sophisticated technologies.

Cellphone cheating

The student uses his or her cellphone to text message the questions from the exam to a friend inside the classroom or outside the testing room. The friend then looks up the answers and sends them back. The student's phone is in silent mode the entire time. Also, the student can enlist a friend enrolled in an earlier section of the same class to take a picture of the exam using a cellphone. The student has time to transfer that photo onto a computer, enlarge it and have all the answers before taking the test.[30]

Online tools

A student must write a paper in a foreign language such as Spanish or French. What should require significant work over several hours is a breeze and can be accomplished in minutes with the help of online language translation services such as Google Language Tools (http://www.google.com/language_tools) or AltaVista Babel Fish Translation (http://babelfish.altavista.com/). The student simply writes the paper in English, pastes it into the translator and then replaces his/her original paper with the results. It may not be perfect although a quick grade of "C" may be better than an earned "A." Other online tools exist to help in various school subjects. For instance, Google also allows users to solve complex mathematical expressions, conversions, and lookup dictionary definitions to name a few (see http://www.google.com/help/features.html). Another website, Math.com includes a variety of tools to help with equations, graphs, inequalities, calculus and more. Cliffs Notes, guides that present and explain literary and other works in pamphlet form are now available online (and for free!; http://www.cliffsnotes.com/).

Gadgets

Some students use handheld computers, calculators with memories, iPods, mp3 players and other gadgets to store formulas, dates, spelling words, and other data likely needed during a test or other learning/assessment activity. The data can be transmitted via infrared or Bluetooth wireless networks to others in the class or even down the hall, through concrete walls. These gadgets are small and may be perceived by adults to be used for purposes other than cheating.

Plagiarism

A 15 year old student got stumped on a summer reading assignment and went to a website (http://www.sparknotes.com) for help. She used its primer to complete the assignment, but never cited the source of the information. Like dozens of other English honors students at her school, she failed the assignment and was accused of plagiarism by her teacher. The alleged plagiarism also highlights the struggle by teachers to keep up with tech-savvy cheaters in the digital age, when term papers can be bought online and the right answer is usually just a mouse click away. [31]

Plagiarism is probably the most misunderstood no-no in the school rulebook. Ask kids what plagiarism means and they usually rattle off "you can't copy right off the Internet or out of a book without identifying the source." When pressed about what exactly that means – like can you copy a sentence, a phrase or a word – most act rather astonished. They have never stopped to think about it and it usually leads to a rather uncomfortable silence. Yet, the consequences of plagiarism can include diminished academic achievement, failing grades, and – in college – being expelled or dismissed from school. So what does plagiarism really mean? [32]

Plagiarism – the attempt to pass off the ideas, research, theories, or words of others as one's own – is a serious academic offense. Most students know when they are intentionally plagiarizing, for example copying an entire essay out of a book or buying a paper off the Internet. Enterprising students can find papers on everything from euthanasia and terrorism to master's-level term papers on biophysics and Shakespeare. Some students lift entire passages from online sites such as http://www.123helpme.com and http://www.CheatHouse.com, where term papers and school projects can be downloaded and copied. According to the Center for Academic Integrity (http://www.academicintegrity.org/), 41% of students admit to "cut and paste" plagiarism and 50% admit to some level of plagiarism from the Internet.

Many kids who plagiarize do so accidentally by not giving proper credit for others' quotes, facts, ideas, or data. Intentional or not, they must still face serious consequences nonetheless. We need to educate our children so that they can save themselves from a great deal of high-tech trouble while respecting the intellectual property rights of others.

There exists a great deal of tips, resources and handouts that you may find helpful in teaching children about the nature of plagiarism (and how to avoid it). Here are a few carefully reviewed websites to help get you started:

Avoiding Plagiarism from the Purdue OWL http://owl.english.purdue.edu/owl/resource/589/03/

How to Avoid Plagiarism from the College Board http://www.collegeboard.com/student/plan/college-success/10314.html

Turnitin Research Resources http://www.turnitin.com/research_site/e_home.html

McGill University Student guide to avoid plagiarism http://www.mcgill.ca/integrity/studentguide/

Prentice Hall: Understanding Plagiarism http://tinyurl.com/2tpp7r

Cracking Software Codes

I didn't realize it until one day I was having problems with a piece of software and searching online for a solution. In my search results I came upon peculiar words like "cracks" and "warez" which caught my attention. As I visited these sites, I quickly realized that what the sites were providing are ways to get around purchasing software, sometimes expensive software. Indeed, this is another form of theft punishable by law.

Software that is highly targeted among "crackers" is usually (a) popular and (b) comes from a company that allows people to download a trial version of its software. A trial version is usually time limited (30 days or so) or has some of the features disabled. If you like the program, you can purchase a code or key that unlocks it and allows it to run without restrictions. Some websites are providing working key codes, key code generators, or re-engineered trial versions that are actually unlocked and fully functioning. [33] Accessing and using software cracks is a much more clear-cut and undeniable example of theft.

In addition to paying hefty fines and facing other criminal consequences, using cracked software can also be problematic in that it often introduces the user to viruses, keylogging software (which logs your keystrokes including passwords to bank accounts or other systems, for example), or other viruses, worms, trojan horses, and bugs. One does not even have to download the modified software, only visit the website on which it is resides and it may automatically begin to download spyware and viruses.

Counter-Cheating Technology

Throughout history, technology has introduced battles between good and evil, right and wrong. Evolving electronics and the Internet affords us very powerful means for accomplishing great things more effectively and efficiently than ever before. At the same time, the same tools are used to wage terror, war, and scandal. A battle between right and wrong is also being waged in the halls and offices of our classrooms in regard to cheating and plagiarism. Students need to be aware that schools are increasingly using high-tech methods to combat cheating. For instance, teachers can ask students to submit their papers in electronic format which they can submit to plagiarism detection services such as http://www.turnitin.com. Affordable software is also beginning to emerge that analyzes student work to determine if students have plagiarized material from the World Wide Web (e.g., see http://www.canexus.com/eve/). Also, schools are banning electronic gadgets such as cell phones and digital cameras from the classroom. Test sites are using surveillance cameras and cell phone signal jammers. Courses that are taught online are incorporating procedures to verify a student's identity throughout the administration of an exam.

GuardingKids.com

What You Can Do

First of all, don't ignore reality. As tempting as it might be to deny that your child would cheat or plagiarize, or to attack his teacher or the school for wrongly accusing him, take a step back. Some parents are simply in denial, and they need to entertain the idea that their kid could be doing this. [34] Awareness of high-tech cheating methods is certainly an important first step in guarding your child against this risk. Take some time to also educate your children/students on the perils of all forms of high-tech theft and the risks in which they put themselves (and you). Also, make sure that they have learned to properly reference the work of others and understand the limitations of using others' words. Encourage kids to pay for and download music, movies, and software from legitimate online services. [35] There are also available plenty of sites that offer legitimate and legal music at no cost such as:

- Amazon.com (http://tinyurl.com/2vw675);
- iTunes free download of the week (http://www.itunes.com); and
- SpiralFrog, a new online music destination, offering ad-supported legal downloads of audio and video content licensed from the catalogs of the world's major and independent record labels (http://www.spiralfrog.com/).
- Also check out Synthopia (http://tinyurl.com/2mrce6) for a list of other sites giving away music mp3s.

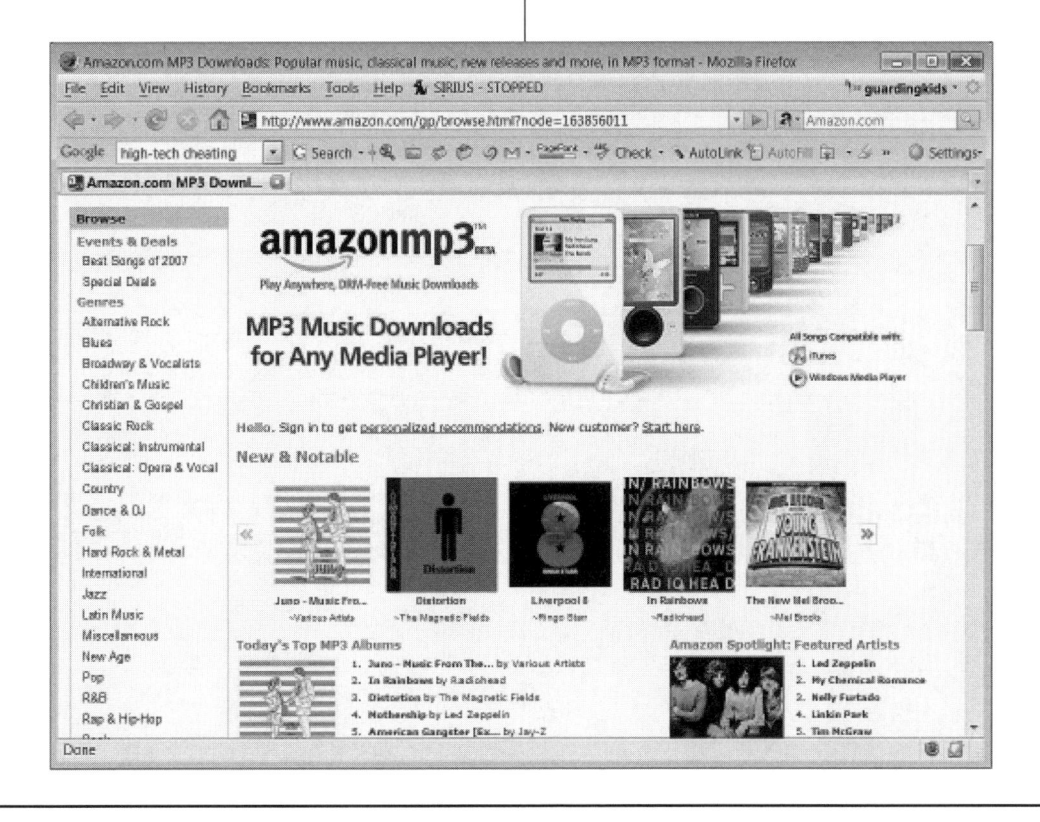

Chapter 4:
Online Communication

Picture you and your child sitting together with Auntie Jane and Uncle Dave when at the dinner table she blurts out, "My Mom said that it's a good thing that you two finally got married and stopped living in sin!" Ahhh .... Woops!

At one time or another, every parent has experienced the horror of their child repeating to others that which was meant to be private. Embarrassing to say the least. Now picture, what if the entire extended family heard the same comment – everyone from cousin Joe in Kalamazoo to his father-in-law, Aldo, in Alabama? Now you are starting to get a picture of what millions of kids are doing everyday – sharing, with anyone who will "listen," their personal stories, fantasies, feelings, sexual escapades, and often times, much, much more. They do this with the same power and efficiency that was once reserved for multi-billion dollar broadcasting networks. They can reach a global audience, including their peers, in a matter of seconds. In addition to e-mail, instant messaging, chat rooms and other mechanisms for electronic communication, this chapter looks at similar tools that go beyond just communicating with others and enters the realm of interactive broadcasting (e.g., through blogs, social networks, and podcasting).

Electronic Mail

Electronic mail has been for some time now the cornerstone for how business and industry disseminates information, communicates, and collaborates with others. This convenient and rapid form of communication, however, is now used among friends and family as a way to conduct business and also stay in touch with loved ones at the touch of a button. Every second of every day we share information, announcements, family photos, and much more. Sometimes even more convenient than picking up the phone, as parents, we are now accustomed to also having the option of communicating with our children's teachers, school principals, soccer coaches, librarians, tutors, and anyone else involved in their lives. Although text messaging is surpassing e-mail in popularity among our kids, e-mail is still a necessary commodity for functioning in modern society. E-mail is everywhere – at our libraries, homes, schools, Internet cafès, and the increasing number of businesses that provide wireless Internet connection while you enjoy their wares or wait for their services (e.g. coffee shops and doctors' offices).

GuardingKids.com

Potential Risk When Using E-mail

Because e-mail is so pervasive in our society, not-so-nice people have used this particular tool to target others for ill purposes. To me, the most reprehensible is how some proliferate links to websites that contain smut and adult material. Worse, sometimes photos and XXX- rated language are included in the e-mail itself. Imagine the effect on your child receiving an e-mail with one of these actual subject lines (known in the pornography industry as "teasers"), "Naked Women Performing Sex with Guns," "Models Get their Fudge Packed," "Pretty Married Mom Waits For You," "Famous victims of parental incest!" or "Welcome to the brutal rape archive!" One question you might ask is, "How do these people find my e-mail address?" the answer is, "It's not that difficult." If you include your e-mail address in an online form when it is you enter a sweepstakes, request information, or sign up for a free account that allows you access to something, your e-mail address may be passed on or sold to others who then send you this filth. Before you enter your e-mail address, consider the reputation of the site and carefully read the sites privacy policy. For example, I have little worry about entering my e-mail address when signing up for free access to the online version of the New York times or for downloading a copy of iTunes. I also feel comfortable entering a sweepstakes conducted by the Home and Garden Television Network (http://www.hgtv.com/) as compared to a completely unfamiliar website. I also know that reputable companies such as Amazon.com take their privacy policy very seriously if they are to continue doing business.

Another way that undesirables obtain your e-mail address is by harvesting it from websites in which it is posted. When you post a comment to an online newsgroup, include your e-mail address in someone's guest book, or when you simply list your e-mail address along with your contact information online, it becomes fair game. Numerous e-mail (and website address) harvesting programs are available to anyone that wants one. These programs, usually very cheap, allow the user to enter key words that it searches for out on the web. If there is an e-mail address on any page that it searches, the program will copy the e-mail address into its database. Within hours, such programs can glean thousands or even millions of e-mail addresses which are then used to send mass unsolicited e-mails. In fact, programs that are designed to send e-mails out very quickly, also known as mass mailers, are also either free or very cheap and easy to come by online. So, be very careful about how your e-mail address ends up online.

To combat e-mail harvesting programs, many companies have moved to online forms which you complete, submit, and then are processed behind the scenes without anyone's e-mail address ever showing up online. Many online groups also allow you to post comments without making your e-mail address available to others. When you need to reply to a member's post, you need to login and complete forms instead of using your own e-mail program. People who maintain websites and still want to include their e-mail address in their contact information are now also posting their e-mail addresses in ways that confuse the harvesting programs. So for instance, instead of posting Sabella@GuardingKids.com, you might see the following "Sabella at guarding kids dot com" which you will have to fix before using it in actual e-mail. Yet others are using a coding format called hexadecimal conversion (e.g., see http://www.u.arizona.edu/~trw/spam/spam.htm) that encodes your e-mail address in such a way that people looking at your site do not see anything different, but a harvesting program looking for your e-mail address cannot see it.

Virtually every company that provides e-mail services and every program that allows you to read and send e-mail now include spam filters and blockers. The problem, however, is that these filters and blockers are not foolproof. Given that there are millions of unsolicited e-mails traveling through cyberspace every second of every day, you are still bound to get a few now and then. The filters and blockers are still no match to human scrutiny and judgments. Although they are great deal of help, you cannot rely on these completely to safeguard your children from inappropriate material.

I Want My Own E-mail Account!

"I want my own television." "I want my own telephone." "I want my own money."... A request that begins with "I want my own ..." is commonplace among households with children. So what will you say when your child asks, "I want my own e-mail account." Allow me to cut to the chase – I believe that there will be times when our children will benefit from the advantages of instant communication. However, I also know that with the power of e-mail comes great responsibility (and risk). Anyone's e-mail account is subject to unsolicited adult material, spam, viruses, phishing scams, and more. Thus my position on e-mail accounts: *Any e-mail account that a child uses is subject to some level of monitoring by a parent.*

The Need for Privacy

Okay, some of you may now have your hands in the air or beating on your chest saying to yourself, "But what about my kids privacy?!" My answer to this is that having a monitored e-mail account does not eliminate a child's privacy. They can still carry on conversations with others via telephone, social gatherings, and in school. Landline (phones connected by a wire at home) and cellular phone plans now include long distance so private conversations are not limited to others in the local community. Another argument for allowing children to have private e-mail access is, "If I don't allow this, they'll just go underground by getting an e-mail account that I don't know about and isn't it better that I know about the account?" I don't think so. In fact, I think this is the same as saying, "I will allow my underage child to smoke and/or drink in my house because if I don't', then they will just do it behind my back without me knowing it and isn't it better that they do it in front of me?" The answer is "no." However, there actually may be some truth to the idea that a child can (and probably will at one time or another) do things like smoke and drink behind your back. For many kids, a bit of experimenting is not uncommon. Ultimately, the decisions they make about these behaviors may have more to do with the relationship you have with them, the kinds of friends that they hang out with, and what they believe about how these behaviors affect them. And if they are doing these things, it still does not justify allowing them to do them at home.

Next, I want to provide you with some options for e-mail accounts that include varying levels of parental monitoring and restrictions. These levels can be viewed across a continuum from least restrictive (e.g., filtered email) to most restive (a shared e-mail account).

Least Restrictive: Use the filtering and other safety features of online web mail accounts.

Moderately Restrictive: Set up an outgoing only e-mail account with all incoming mail being forwarded to your accounts.

Most Restrictive: Set up an e-mail account that only you can log into and review all emails together.

Email

Least Restrictive ← → Most Restrictive

Least Restrictive: Filtered E-mails Accounts

The least restrictive level of e-mail independence is what I call the filtered e-mail account. That is, you allow your child to use an e-mail client or service that accommodates various levels of control. One of my favorites is an e-mail service that allows incoming e-mails from only those people listed in one's address book. If the e-mail is from someone not in the address book, it is either put in a folder for review or flagged as Junk and automatically deleted. Hotmail (http://www.hotmail.com), a free e-mail service from Microsoft Corporation, allows for this feature and is worth a look.

Here's how you do it with Hotmail.com ...

1. Set up your Hotmail account by visiting http://www.hotmail.com
2. Click on the *Options* link and then *More Options*
3. Click on *Junk e-mail* and then *Filters and Reporting*
4. Under Choose a junk e-mail filter, choose *Exclusive - Everything is sent to the junk e-mail folder except messages from your contacts and safe senders, Windows Live Hotmail service announcements, and alerts that you signed up for.*
5. Under Delete junk e-mail choose *Immediately - Junk e-mail is deleted immediately.*

Moderately Restrictive: Monitored E-mail Accounts

Okay, I know that when it comes to teenagers and for kids whom at this point have enjoyed their own private e-mail account, it would be very difficult to take it away. You might need some compromise. How about an e-mail account that your child owns although is minimally monitored by you. When I say minimally monitored, I mean that you review e-mails coming *in* to the account although not necessarily going out of the account. The message to the child is, *"I trust you when it comes to you sending information/message to others although I must be able to see how the outside world may be trying to communicate with you."*

Here's how you do it ....

1. You need to have an e-mail service that has "send a copy to (address)" options. The best thing to do is to purchase a domain and web host service which is about $5-10 per month and comes with e-mail accounts (e.g., webstrikesolutions.com).
2. Then, go into the administration or control panel that allows you to set up e-mail.
3. Make sure to put your own e-mail address in the "send a copy to" field.
4. Any e-mail sent to your child's account will also go to yours.

Another tip ... in the e-mail program (also called client) that your child is using, you can also check the option that saves a copy of all Sent e-mails to a folder (usually named Sent). Once in a while you can review all sent e-mail as well. Although, know that this option can easily be unchecked and e-mails in the Sent folder can always be deleted so doing this may not be reliable.

By the way, there is another advantage of monitoring incoming messages. When your child signs up for various accounts (e.g., online video, games, etc.) and uses her e-mail to do it, you should receive a confirmation e-mail that alerts you to the event and often gives you the logon information (i.e., userid and password).

Most Restrictive: Controlled E-mail Accounts

Simply put, a controlled e-mail account is one in which only the adult knows the password and can access the account. The adult and child process the e-mail together.

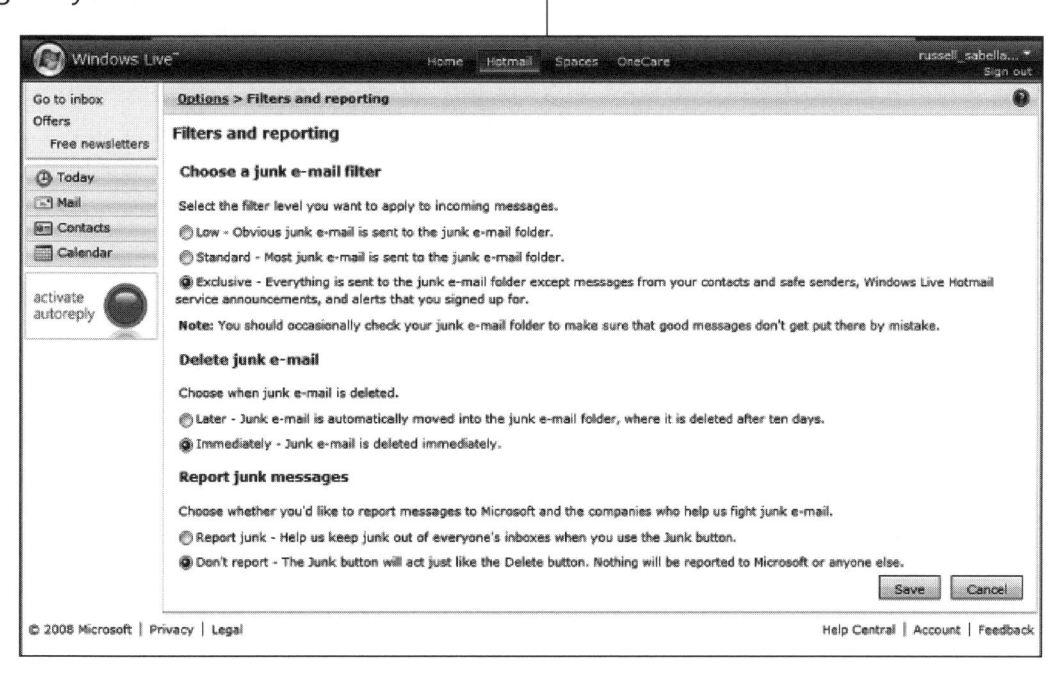

Chat Rooms

Chat rooms are located throughout the Web and focus on countless topics. Most chat rooms are social gathering places where children, and especially teens, congregate to talk about whatever they want. Essentially, conversations traditionally occurring in the school lunchroom, hallways, and parking lots are now online without the limitations of actually being present. By using an online chat room, children can meet others with an online connection anywhere on the planet and at any time during the day or night. Oftentimes chat sessions happen at the same time that a student may be doing his or her homework, moving back and forth from work to play and play to work. This is the first issue that parents need to watch out for as this type of multi-tasking may introduce just enough distraction to hinder a child from academically succeeding. Upon closer inspection of chat rooms, parents will also find other possible threats to their children's well being.

Chat rooms are not always filled with innocent and playful conversation. Some children will use the convenience of a chat room to say hateful things about their peers and, over time, release a relentless barrage of harassment and bullying – whether their target is present in the chat room or not. In other words, chat rooms extend the ability of some children to bad mouth other children and sometimes adults such as their teachers. With the almost instantaneous speed of electronic communication, ugly rumors can easily gain momentum and spill over into the classroom. Some rumors may even lead to physical confrontations among the participants as well as emotional distress or depression among victims (more on that later when I cover cyberbullying). Another illicit use of chat rooms involves how predators or child molesters can use this technology to lure and kidnap children for their own deviant interests. Predators may easily disguise themselves behind the veil of anonymity afforded by electronic communication, select their target, develop a trusting relationship with them, and slowly begin more isolated or private chats with their victims. This is not difficult to do because most chat rooms have what's called a "private" or "whisper" function which allows any individual to chat one-on-one with anyone else. Some children and teens use the same identity and will frequent a particular chat room that they like very often. Sometimes, chat room participants can learn to depend on some chat room users who log in on an almost daily basis and at the same time – usually after school or before going to bed. Predators many "lurk" to determine which participant will make the easiest target based on their age, apparent level of self-confidence, and willingness to maintain secrecy. Once their victim is selected, the predator may also move the conversation over to e-mail, telephone, or even videoconferencing. Sometimes predators will also go so far as giving money to a child so that he or she may purchase phone cards and call without being detected. Similarly, a predator may help a child purchase a post office box to discreetly receive letters and gifts. With the power of the Internet, predators can now also use stolen credit cards to purchase airline flights, rental cars, and hotel rooms to meet their victims without being easily detected.

One online chat room, http://www.stickam.com/, can be particularly troublesome because it allows any group of users to chat using both live video and audio in addition to simple text. Multiple people can see, hear, and interact in real time using only a common computer, Internet connection, and webcam.

Check out these other chatrooms as an example of how children may chat online. I encourage you to log in (as a guest user if possible so that you don't have to bother registering for an account) and just read (without interacting) for a while to get a better sense of what some kids may be up to:

http://www.ecrush.com/

http://www.chat-avenue.com/kidchat.html

http://www.kidchatters.com/ (This one requires parental registration and is monitored as well as filtered).

http://www.kidscom.com/chat/kidschat/kidschat.html

http://www.kidzworld.com/

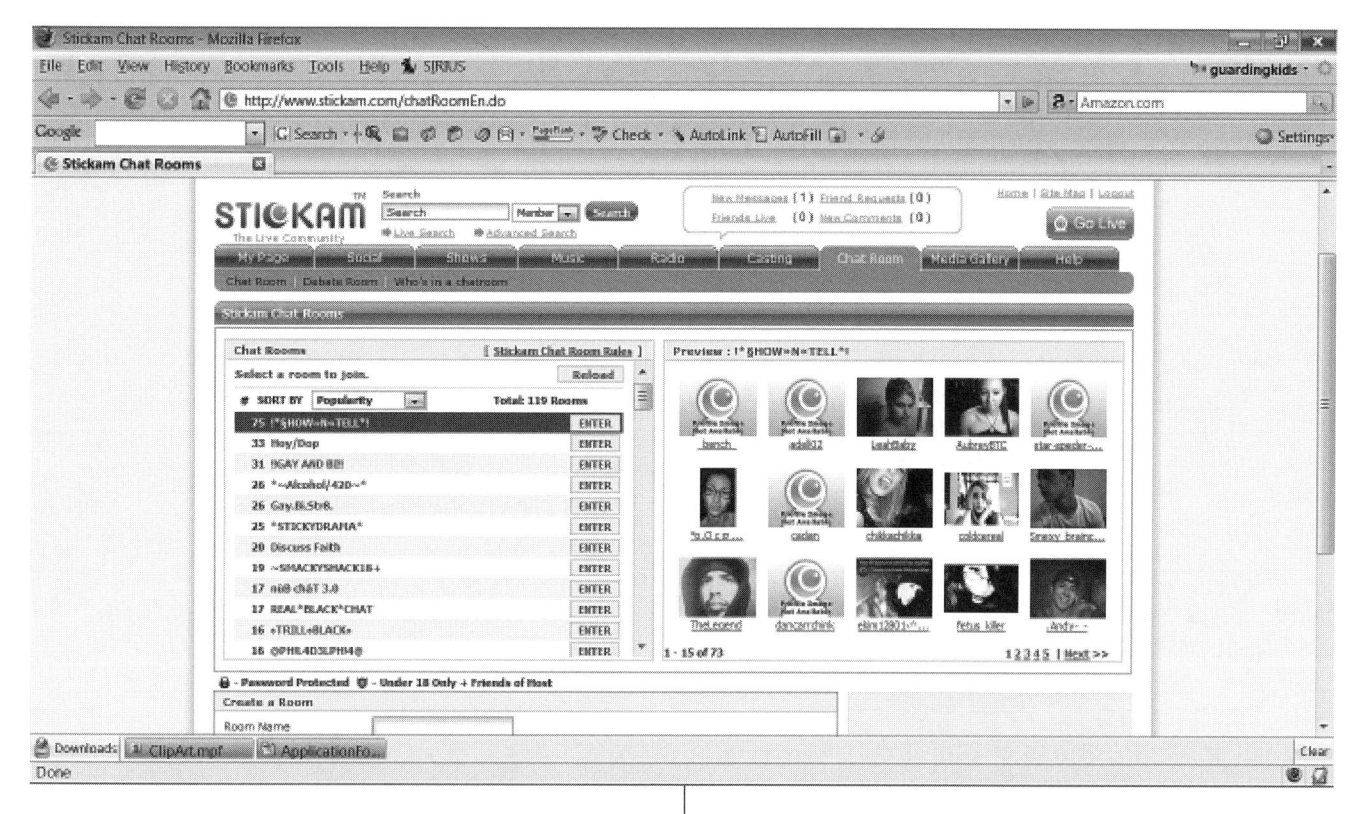

Instant Messaging

For many years, e-mail was the most popular application on the Internet—a popular and "sticky" communications method that keeps users coming back day after day. But e-mail has shown a slow decline among online teens who have begun to express a preference for instant messaging (IM) programs such as MSN Messenger, Yahoo! Messenger, ICQ (short for "I Seek You"), or AOL Instant Messenger (AIM) to send Instant Messages to one another. According to one study conducted by the Pew Internet & American Life Project, when asked about which modes of communication they use most often when communicating with friends, online teens consistently choose IM over e-mail in a wide array of contexts. Teens who participated in focus groups for this study said that they view e-mail as something you use to talk to "old people," institutions, or to send complex instructions to large groups. When it comes to casual written conversation, particularly when talking with friends, online instant messaging is the clearly the mode of choice for today's online teens. If you have used IM, you can understand why this is true as it's a pretty "cool" and fun thing to do.

Instant messaging has become the digital communication backbone of teens' daily lives. About half of instant-messaging teens — or roughly 32% of all teens — use IM every single day. As the platforms for instant messaging programs spread to cell phones and handheld devices, teens are starting to take textual communication with them into their busy and increasingly mobile lives. IM is a staple of teens' daily Internet diet and is used for a wide array of tasks — to make plans with friends, talk about homework assignments, joke around, check in with parents, and post "away messages" or notices about what they are doing when they are away from their computers. The good news is that instant messaging and text messaging are not simply used for conversations with other tech-savvy peers. Almost one in three (29%) teens who use IM or text messaging will use it to communicate with their parents.

So what exactly is instant messaging? Basically, instant messaging is an Internet-based group conversation that includes all the benefits of chat rooms and so much more. Users organize groups of friends into "buddy lists," with everyone choosing a unique screen name. Whenever you log on, you can instantly see who else from your group is online at that time. You simply send a message and instantly join in the conversation. It's really a private chat room for a group of friends. Although two-way conversations are possible, usually everyone in the group joins in. Other features include the ability to transmit voice and video, send files (especially music and video), and provide links to websites.

When it comes to our kids, instant messaging poses the same threats as does communicating via online chat rooms although does have some added threats which you should be aware of. For one, if your child is on the buddy list of another IM user, perhaps someone with ulterior motives, the other user will immediately be alerted when your child logs in. The user no longer needs to wait around and watch for a potential target to login. Once an identified target logs in to the instant messaging environment, a "doorbell" begins to ring on the computer.

According to some social scientists, another aspect of instant messaging that is worrisome is how this tool may hinder our youth from learning appropriate social skills by actually interacting with other kids in the real world. How might socializing in chat rooms ultimately have a negative impact on self-confidence? Young people often find IM easier than talking face to face. For instance, a girl who normally gets tongue-tied around boys can easily carry on a conversation using typed words and "emoticons" or "smileys" to convey messages. This eliminates awkward conversational pauses, embarrassing fumbles for the right words, and the more intimidating aspects of face-to-face encounters. Could this, however, be robbing her of developing important social skills? Or could it be that socializing in chat rooms provides safety training for the real world? More research is needed to answer these questions more definitely. In the meantime, my vote is to error on the side of caution and minimize the use of IM chatting, especially when it seems to interfere with opportunities for real life social development.

According to the Los Angeles County District Attorney's Office (http://da.co.la.ca.us/pok/im.htm), a third aspect of instant messaging which can put kids at risk has to do with them divulging personal information. Besides offering real-time contact with strangers or others who may seek to harm your child, Instant Messaging allows for the immediate dissemination of significant personal information. When your child signs up for an IM account, he or she is asked to fill out a personal profile that asks for key identifying information on the account holder. This personal profile may then be placed in an Internet directory that can be viewed by all. The directory can be searched by name, date of birth, gender, and interests. Consequently, an unsuspecting child can effectively place himself or herself in a position to receive unsolicited offers of sex, pornography, and other dubious material.

Also ...

Youth workers note that IM can be time-consuming—and even addictive.

You can receive pornographic "spam" through your instant messaging program.

You may receive computer viruses via file transfers that are not scanned by anti-virus software.

Instant Messaging programs now allow for file sharing which makes it very easy to introduce rich adult content and illegal downloads.

Video Communications

A combination of web cameras (also known as webcams) and the Internet can spell trouble if mixed with youthful enthusiasm and naivete. For example, a type of pornography that can be found on the Web is live "video conferencing" in which the "caller" interacts with one or more individuals who perform sexual activities at the prompting of the user. These live shows vary from the tame to the lewd, and can include any number of users all typing or speaking commands simultaneously. One of the most recent examples of this in the media is the case of Justin Berry. Justin (born in 1986) is an American who operated a child pornography Internet site featuring his own erotic performances beginning at the age of 13. Over the course of five years, more than 1,500 people paid Berry to appear naked and engage in sex acts on camera. In the process of operating his for-pay sites, he met several of his website's members in real life, accepted money and gifts from them and later raised allegations of molestation by them. Berry abandoned his business in 2005 and became a witness for both federal and state investigators in a large scale child pornography investigation. Berry's national notoriety was increased by his February 15, 2006 appearance on The Oprah Winfrey Show and other appearances, first on C-SPAN while testifying before Congress, and later for an interview on Larry King Live. In his interview with Kurt Eichenwald, a New York Times reporter, Berry stated that at age 13 he began receiving offers of gifts from adults in exchange for disrobing on webcam. He was first offered $50 for removing his shirt. "I figured, I took off my shirt at the pool for nothing, so, I was kind of like, what's the difference?" After that he set up a wish list on Amazon.com and received items from the list in exchange for webcam performances. Requests for Berry to perform on camera gradually became more explicit at the request of viewers, progressing from full frontal nudity to masturbation. In his Congressional testimony, Berry said that the effort to convince him to fully disrobe on camera was slow, and that at age 13, "the horror of what was happening did not strike me." [36]

Webcams should only be used with *direct* supervision when, for example, interacting with family and friends at a distance. When finished, I recommend parents disconnect and secure the webcam for future supervised uses. Also, look out for future technology such as video conferencing over cell phones to pose some of the same risks as webcams do now.

Online Videos

Sharing video through online services has become a true phenomenon. One of the most popular, YouTube.com, originally started as a personal video sharing service and has grown into an entertainment destination with people watching videos more than 100 million times a day. It is no wonder given how easy it is these days to upload a video. With digital video cameras and video phones, most kids can figure out how to capture video, do some basic editing, and upload within a short time. Not too long ago a news reporter in my community showed how easy it was to track a teen down after she uploaded a short video to YouTube. The teen did a good job of not displaying personal information that could lead to her identity and location but did forget one thing: you shouldn't include your full name at the end of the movie while the credits are rolling. Perhaps it wasn't even her that did the movie editing and whoever did do it wasn't thinking (or didn't care). The video was also shot in and around her house so it wasn't difficult to narrow her house down within a neighborhood. All one had to do was look for the large trampoline in her backyard, the one surrounded by a chain link fence. And because Florida includes a great deal of information about it's citizens online, the news reporter only had to put the kid's last name into a government database, get her address, and start scouting the location. Her parents were mortified when the investigative reporter knocked on their door.

Another way that online videos can introduce trouble is when someone captures on video someone else doing something that is against school rules, house rules, or even the law. This is happening now quite a bit on social networks such as Facebook and MySpace. Kids are recording footage of school fights, arson, drunken behavior, and lewd conduct.

In fact, there now exists lingo such as a "bully bang", "uvv (ultra violent video) sweep", "happy slapping", or "fast slapping" to describe when a thug sneaks up on a victim, beats them quickly, captures it all on a cell phone camera, and then posts the humiliating punishment on the web to shame and terrify the victim. Others view the video, pass it along to their friends via e-mail or blog posting, and the damaging effects multiplies. [37] In addition to YouTube.com, you may also want to check out other video sharing sites. Google the words "share online video" [no quotes] and you'll begin to see just how many there are available. Also, if you want to learn more about the nature of online video sharing, you can download and read a report entitled *Increased Use of Video-sharing Sites* conducted by the Pew Internet & American Life Project available online at http://www.pewinternet.org/PPF/r/232/report_display.asp.

Telephony

One of my favorite commercials is one where a teenager was apparently in trouble and grounded from using the telephone. Next thing you know, we see her in her bedroom sitting in front of her computer, talking to one of her friends anyway. Her mom walks in, sees her in front of the computer, and assumes that she is working. Mom gives her a big smile and walks out closing the door behind her. I've already mentioned before that kids can talk with others through chat rooms and instant messaging. But there's more ... Anyone can now talk to anyone else anywhere in the world without even picking up a phone. With the advent of "Voice Over Internet Protocol or VOIP (also known as telephony)," our voice is converted from analog to digital and streamed to someone else's computer or even telephone! Services such as Skype (http://www.skype.com) make this available for free and they're not the only ones out there. [38]

Blogs

You've probably heard the term blog more than once, most likely used on television or print news media. However, you may still not exactly understand what a blog is. According to the Webopedia (see http://www.webopedia.com/TERM/b/blog.html), a blog, short for "web log", is a web page that serves as a publicly accessible personal journal for an individual. Typically updated on a daily basis, blogs often reflect the personality of the author. Google owned Blogger.com describes a blog as, "A blog is a personal diary. A daily pulpit. A collaborative space. A political soapbox. A breaking-news outlet. A collection of links. Your own private thoughts. Memos to the world."

Creating a blog is simple and free. It only takes a few minutes by entering your name, e-mail address and a few other pieces of (usually personal) information. Some blogs ask for the users age and others do not. For those that do, the system does not provide age verification services so faking one's age is a matter of putting in the right birth date. You select "the look" (template) of your blog from a set of standard options, click a few buttons, and another blog has been added to the "blogosphere." Once the blog is set up, a child can post text, links, audio and video to their hearts delight. From their computer or cell phone, they can say or show anything and everything. With a bit of know-how, they can even easily syndicate to other blogs and websites. Syndication is a process by which the latest content from a blog, or from any other web page, can be made available for re-publication in another website or in some other application. Syndication is easily achieved through free online services that provide what are called RSS (real simple syndication) feeds.[39] And millions of children are doing it. According to the Pew Internet & American Life Project report entitled *Teen Content Creators and Consumers* (2005), at least 8 million teens blog, which is probably an underestimation since those statistics were collected a while ago, and the numbers might be higher if you factor in not just blogs but the world of social websites, especially the booming MySpace, which includes blog capabilities.

In a nutshell, a typical blog has a main page and nothing else. On the main page, there is a set of entries. Each entry is a little text blurb that may contain embedded links out to other sites, news stories, etc. When the author adds a new entry, it goes at the top, pushing all the older entries down. Blogs can also have a right sidebar that contains additional permanent links to other sites and stories. The author might update the sidebar weekly or monthly. The technology that allows individuals (or companies, especially news agencies) to write one's own blog is so relatively simple and inexpensive that it is no surprise that they have proliferated the Web as fast as they have.

How Kids Create Their Own Blogs

Any kid can create basic blogs for free through one or more online services, and most of these toolsets have additional features available for a small fee. Here are just a few of the services available.

- **Blogger** (http://www.blogger.com/): Free, automated web log publishing platform in one easy to use website.

- **BBlog** (http://www.bblog.com/): bBlog is a powerful, elegant personal publishing system written in PHP and released as free, Open Source software under the GPL. It is a flexible but simple way to blog that works for blogging beginners, and can grow into a more advanced user's needs.

- **TypePad** (http://www.typepad.com/): Similar to blogger, another blogging service although this one has a minimal cost.

- **LiveJournal** (http://www.livejournal.com/): Joining this service site is free although users can choose to upgrade their accounts for extra features.

- **Moveable Type** (http://www.movabletype.com/): "The perfect platform for building easy-to-maintain blog, web, and social media sites."

- **MySpace.com** (http://www.myspace.com/): Actually a hybrid site that allows people to post their personal interests, write blogs, put up video and set up ways to communicate with their friends boasted over 220 million users as of late January, 2008.

- **Wordpress.com** (http://wordpress.com): "You can get a blog started in less time than it takes you to read this sentence. All you need is an e-mail address and a name. You can blog as much as you want for free, your blog can be public to the world or private for just your friends, and our paid upgrades are completely optional."
- **Xanga** (http://www.xanga.com/): a community of online diaries and journals.

I want to reiterate one more time at this point something I don't want us all to forget. Blogs, like any other technology, is neither good or evil. How this tool is used and for what purpose determines its value. In fact, blogs are closely being explored for how they can make a positive difference in education (for instance, see http://oedb.org/library/features/top-100-education-blogs and http://edublogs.org/).

Podcasting

Podcasting, in its basic form, involves creating audio files (most commonly in MP3 format) and making them available online in a way that allows users to automatically download the files for listening at their leisure (this is known as subscribing to the podcast). After subscribing to the podcast, any new audio files are automatically download to your computer which can then be transferred easily to a handheld device such as a Palm OS Handheld, a Pocket PC, cell phone, or an iPod - hence, the name Podcast. In essence, anyone with a computer, Internet access, free software, and a microphone can turn their computer into a personal studio and produce their very own radio show/program. [40]

Relatively speaking, podcasting is still in its infancy although shows no signs of abatement. Hundreds of podcasts are added to the Internet every day. One reason for their popularity is that producing a podcast is relatively cheap. Podcasting requires no more hardware or software than a typical computer user has. Second, the MP3 files and accompanying text which are served over the World Wide Web are supported among virtually all operating systems (i.e., podcasting works across many platforms including Microsoft Windows and Apple Macintosh). As a result, these types of files have become quite pervasive. Third, given the difficulties and intricacies of using computer technology sometimes, podcasting is surprisingly simple to do. Only three steps are required (create the MP3 file, upload the file, and update your RSS feed) to broadcast any content you would like. A fourth reason that podcasting is so popular is that it removes barriers of space, pace, and time by allowing the consumer to download and listen to broadcasts at his or her convenience (sort of like Tivo® for radio). And, the consumer may listen to a broadcast using various devices such as computers, MP3 players, CD players (after burning the files to a CD), personal digital assistants (PDA's), Bluetooth or USB enabled radios, and now cell phones. Finally, I have found that podcasting is just plain fun. Whether adult or child, podcasting helps the user join more closely than ever the ranks of other popular radio show hosts, DJ's, and personalities.

As you may have already guessed, the major disadvantage related to podcasting is that, like everything else on the Internet, podcasts are not regulated. Pornographers, bigots, bullies, and others have also discovered podcasts as a powerful method for disseminating information. Plus, whereas most podcasts use simple audio, more and more have turned to video podcasting or V-casting. Anyone who has the knowledge, including children, can easily access (and/or produce) a wide range of smut or obscene material. In fact, there exists many websites such as http://iporndirectory.com/ and http://ipod.handheldpornsites.com that provide pornography download services just for iPods and similar devices. Thus, the development of podcasting emphasizes once again the importance of media and technology literacy among youth and adults alike. Evaluating, choosing, and using appropriate information presents challenges that, if not managed, can leave us unbalanced, unfocused, and in a state of deterioration.

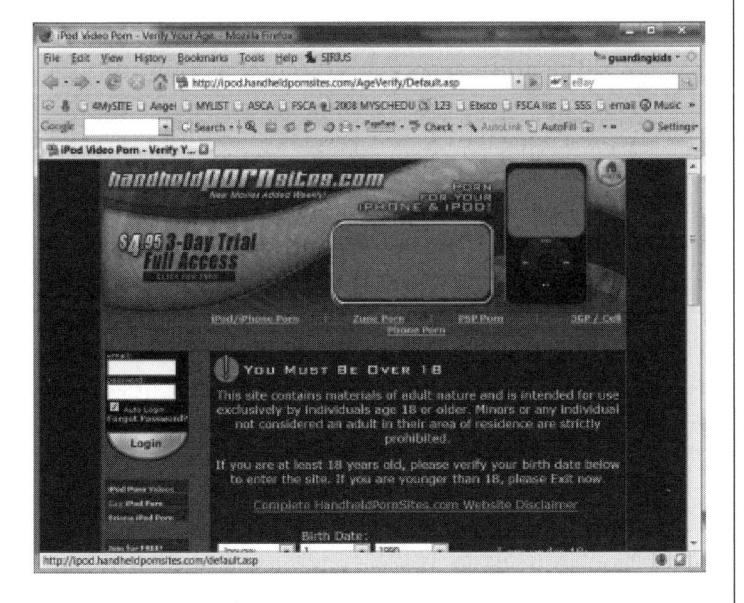

Internet Social Networks

Social networking, among other things, refers to a category of Internet applications to help connect friends, business partners, or other individuals together using a variety of tools. Social networking sites go beyond posting information and allowing others to post comments. They facilitate the connection to other users with similar interests. Until now, these networks were primarily designed for use among adults for both professional and personal fulfillment. For business and industry, social networks connects buyers and sellers, employers and prospects, and otherwise facilitates the sharing of business opportunities. These networks can grow very quickly and be quite effective at making important business contacts. For example, on the Spoke Website (http://www.spoke.com), a user completes a simple personal profile (e.g name, title, company, contact information) and then clicks a button marked "build network." A program is then downloaded from the Spoke website that mines the user's Microsoft Outlook e-mail and contact database for information about who he/she knows and how frequently he/she maintains contact with them. In a few minutes, the user's new, online "Spoke book'" is populated not only with the hundreds or thousands of contacts he/she had manually entered into his/her Outlook contacts list, but also with everyone she/he had ever exchanged e-mail with from that e-mail account. Spoke also rates the strength of these relationships based on how often and how recently the user e-mailed with each person, as well as whether he/she was the only recipient of a message or was simply part of a larger distribution list.

During the same time that social networks were being developed among business and industry, a more personal – *much* more personal – social network was also gaining popularity. Online dating services or relationship sites were, at first, a bit awkward and frankly hard to believe. I remember the sentiment in the mid 1990's, "How could it be that a person could actually find their future spouse, his or her life partner – the person with whom they will be so very highly intimate with – by first 'meeting' via text communication and photographs? How can this be done without first making contact in person, or even on the phone? What if the person is a predator, sexual deviant, rapist, criminal – who knows who these people really are?" Some concerns still exist in the online dating world of today. However, they have become mainstream as compared to only ten or eleven short years ago when this service was seen as useful only for "geeks," "loners," or, for some other reason, the "undatable." Today, personal matching networks such as eHarmony.com, Match.com, lavalife.com, chemistry.com, matchmaker.com, Yahoo! Personals, and date.com have millions of members who seek to make romantic connections, some of which result in marriage and others of which find their way in the better forgotten annals of dating history.

It was only a matter of time before youngsters, especially teenagers, discover the power of the Internet to foster peer relations – the staple of adolescence. It goes something like this: Johnny can connect with Sally, a "friend," and explore her list of friends. Johnny notices Jennifer who catches his fancy and invites her to become one of his "friends." Sally then explores John's list, invites Adam to be a friend, and this is how the network grows exponentially. MySpace.com, the largest social networking site currently available, describes social networking in his way:

"Once you have your profile up and running, start inviting your friends to join in on the fun. By building your personal network, you can start expanding your circle of friends exponentially. Encourage your friends to invite their friends ... Learn their interests, read their online journals, and view their pictures. Browse through everyone's "Friends List" and see whom you are connected to. You'll be amazed at all the interesting people you are associated with through networks of mutual friends!"

In fact, social networking sites continue to get increasingly sophisticated including video, audio, instant chat, voice messages, classifieds, e-mailing, file swapping, links, voting, and much more. Other popular social networks include: [41]

❏ **Facebook**. Facebook is made up of many networks, each based around a company, region, or school. Join the networks that reflect your real-life communities to learn more about the people who work, live, or study around you. http://www.facebook.com/

❏ **Faceparty**. This site also has an adult section which can only be accessed with adult verification. http://www.faceparty.com/

❏ **Friendster**. This one also adds the ability to share unlimited personal files - especially video and photos - with your friends. http://www.friendster.com/

❏ **hi5**. While on hi5, members discover friends, artists, and content. hi5 provides a platform for established artists, underground talent, and everyday people to all gain prominence amongst a worldwide audience. Members voice their opinions and increase the significance of an artist, a person, or a piece of content. http://www.hi5.com/

- **Piczo.** This site uses free form tools which makes it super easy to have a website up and running within minutes. It also seems to cater exclusively to children, especially of late elementary or middle school ages. http://www.piczo.com/

- **Tickle.** According to the company, the Tickle Social Network is the first social networking product to deliver deep user profiles that go beyond basic demographic data to include group affiliations, career history, and personality traits. http://connect.tickle.com/

- **Xanga.** Xanga is a community of online diaries and journals. You can easily start your own free journal, share thoughts with your friends and meet new friends, too! http://www.xanga.com/

So What's the Problem with Kids and Social Networking?

According to one *USA Today* report by Janet Kornblum, unprecedented numbers of teens are using blogs to do what they once did through personal diaries, phone conversations and hang-out sessions: cementing friendships with classmates, seeking new friends, venting, testing social limits, getting support and getting all *emo* ("highly emotional" in blog-speak). [42] Kornblum writes that, "Blogs and social sites are so popular that many schools have banned them. Just last week a private school in New Jersey took it a step further, telling students to dismantle their personal Internet diaries or face suspension." Why all the hoopla? It's simple: kids are revealing to the rest of the world information that is inappropriate and too personal, especially information that can make it easy for a predator to identify, track, and lure the youngster. Teens and tweens (tweens are kids who are kind of in between being a grade schooler and a teenager) are regularly revealing everything from where they attend school to where they live, work, play, hang out, and study. Many also include photos of themselves and their friends taken in their house, or worse, in their rooms in full view of posters and other personal items – useful information about interests that can be used for evil motives.

Some mental health and psychology professionals wonder, "Are social networks being used by depressed kids to interact with others and isolating them even further from the real world? Has social networking become a poor substitute for professional counseling?" It may be that children who are in pain or in need are turning to technologies such as blogging, podcasting, and social networking to better cope. Therapists are beginning to realize this. The following e-mail was posted over a counseling related listserv from a professor and counselor who has learned to incorporate students' Facebook pages into their treatment: [43]

I started a practice late last spring that I intend to continue, as an experiment, this fall. When students are referred for an alcohol screening - both mandated and self referrals - I would check to see if the student had a Facebook.com page. If the student had a page, I would review it to get a sense of how the student sees him or herself, especially in regard to high-risk behaviors. True to what we learn from social norming data that have been published, most - the vast majority - of student pages I have reviewed have been in what I refer to as the, "PG or PG-13" rated range. There have been, however, a couple with comments, nicknames and/or photos attached that have suggested rather high-risk behavior practices.

Since anyone with a .edu e-mail address can open an account in the facebook.com, this might be a useful tool for those who do screenings. I have found the tool to be useful in exploring the apparent inconsistencies in a student's self-reports on personal preferences and behavior and the student's facebook.com page when I conduct an assessment. Perhaps it is my white beard and an obviously middle-aged if not grandfatherly appearance that lets me get away with this, but I find that feigning my best impersonation of Peter Faulk as Columbo, as I act befuddled, touching my forehead saying, "Help me understand something...I seem to be a bit confused here...but you just told me 'X' about your approach to socializing, yet when I looked at your facebook page, it seems to suggest something different. Help me sort out what's what." Obviously, there cannot be any condescension in one's voice when employing this strategy and in true motivational interviewing style, one should never argue with a client, but it has been interesting to see how the facebook may become another tool that is useful in attempting to engage a student in a realistic conversation about personal choices related to drinking.

As an aside - and I have not done this as yet - it occurs to me that the facebook, or should I say, student entries about themselves IN the facebook, may also be useful when addressing issues related to self-esteem, self-respect, students concerns about how they are perceived, etc. By talking about how students refer to themselves in their entries, e.g., the language they use, the images they post, etc., we may be able to invite students to recognize that we all teach others how we should be treated by the way we present ourselves in public. This is sort of like what a career counselor might due when explaining that a student might want to consider changing his or her e-mail address on a resume from "thekegmeister@whatever.com."

Just a thought to start some discussion at the start of another academic year.

Best regards,

Dr. Robert Chapman

Sometimes, simply getting stuff "off your chest" can help you feel better and lead to real improvement (this is called catharsis in counseling terms). This may especially be true if a child feels isolated and/or lonely and begins to see that his peers show signs of empathy or understanding about his situation. Oftentimes, however – especially when a child suffers from some mental disorder or serious psychological/social issues – it does not. Parents should keep in mind that some children may attempt to use online disclosures as a substitute for more appropriate and effective professional help. Also, similar to how Dr. Chapman uses Facebook to gather extra information about a student he works with in treatment, parents can use their children's online postings as a focus of conversation with the intent to advance a connection, foster trust and provide timely guidance (as opposed to espionage and interrogation).

Another problem with social networks occurs when some kids post information online that is derogatory or mean-spirited. This is one very good reason why schools are legitimately concerned over potential liability for personal blogging on school computers during recess and study halls. In some cases, children target school personnel such as teachers and administrators. At the very least, this is inappropriate. Worse, it could be a violation of school policy (most schools now have Acceptable Use Policies [AUP] when it comes to computer and Internet use). [44] Even worse, it could be criminal based on state or federal terroristic threat laws. Students could get expelled or criminally charged. Consider that two 10th grade girls at one high school confessed to making an online death threat against other students. They say it was a joke. But they are now facing delinquency criminal charges. School district officials found out about the threats after other students read the posting. Some called a school hotline to report it. Others told the principal the next morning.

In seemingly more frequent cases, disparaging comments are exchanged among peers or other students. This can happen when a child relays his or her opinion and another child does not agree and a "flame war" ensues. A flame war is the deliberate exchange of insults between two or more people, usually over an electronic medium such as listserv, chatroom, instant messenger, blog or website. The message itself is called a "flame" and the author is said to be "flaming."

Here is a real example of a chat room transcript (personally identifying information deleted):

7:06 PM: lil_hottie (guest): mi sis iz no punk she doznt even like punk boyz I think?

7:06 PM: punkclowns (guest): yo she didnt have to call me names when people do that I really do get a little sad

7:07 PM: punkclowns (guest): check out my pictures on my site and you tell me whant you think

7:07 PM: lil_hottie (guest): ok then I just mouth them on and mi sis doz a sure good damn job @ it............. lol

7:07 PM: lil_hottie (guest): I get it 4um her................lol

7:08 PM: lil_hottie (guest): ya ic the pics...........

7:08 PM: lil_hottie (guest): wut 4 ???

7:08 PM: punkclowns (guest): yo your parents suck at razing you and you just a peace of trash in the world

********** at 7:08 PM lil_hottie (guest) left the room

********** at 7:09 PM lil_hottie (guest) joined the room

********** The messages above were sent before you arrived.

GuardingKids.com

lil_hottie (guest): no im not wut the f did I do

lil_hottie (guest): brb

********** at 7:10 PM lil_hottie (guest) left the room

********** at 7:10 PM lil_hottie (guest) joined the room

punkclowns (guest): you said you mouf off people you sound like a damb bully

lil_hottie (guest): well if there rude to me I will I don't take no cumin out of sum bitches that go on here tho...............so

lil_hottie (guest): thats wut I meant

punkclowns (guest): you know im the nicest guy youll meet but your sis was a jerk so you any no better you even said you learn from here

punkclowns (guest): don't call me a bitch

lil_hottie (guest): I wasnt the bitches(gurls)that cum on here

lil_hottie (guest): bitches r girls ya no like females

punkclowns (guest): fine just don't call me nuthin

lil_hottie (guest): k then

lil_hottie (guest): u want me 2 call ya nuthin?

punkclowns (guest): dam im mad at you too

lil_hottie (guest): nvm

lil_hottie (guest): y I didnt call you n/e thing

punkclowns (guest): is your sis who started it

punkclowns (guest): and don't tell me she not meen

lil_hottie (guest): k I no w.e it s over now forget about it

punkclowns (guest): k ty

punkclowns (guest): you sound way nicer

lil_hottie (guest): thnx but don't push it cuz I aint dat nice...........lol

lil_hottie (guest): k

punkclowns (guest): check out my picture on sight though and honestlyy tell me how I look

lil_hottie (guest): well I do follow her cuz I aint lett'n no1 mouth mi sis off..............kk

punkclowns (guest): k

punkclowns (guest): go to site tell me how I look

lil_hottie (guest): just to let ya no b4 I check it I don't like punks..................so

punkclowns (guest): one or two picks are punk but that was just for fun

punkclowns (guest): im not even aloud to do mohawks anymore

punkclowns (guest): so go ahead

lil_hottie (guest): and I don't like clowns either I don't think ne gurl doz

lil_hottie (guest): w.e

punkclowns (guest): I not a clown

lil_hottie (guest): well ur name.............explain cuz it don't seem so kool lol

punkclowns (guest): hurry check my mom here

lil_hottie (guest): well I cant

lil_hottie (guest): so ....

punkclowns (guest): oh I made a comedy website so you know just for fun

lil_hottie (guest): no thnx...............lol

punkclowns (guest): already saw your site please check my photo

lil_hottie (guest): well????

punkclowns (guest): nice

lil_hottie (guest): no

lil_hottie (guest): I didnt go on it

lil_hottie (guest): and n/e wayz...........

GuardingKids.com

These two individuals, a boy and a girl in early middle school, have never met in person. This is their first meeting and online conversation. From the looks of it, hopefully their last.

Why is online communication at risk for getting ugly? This is a topic currently researched in the social and computer sciences, typically called computer mediated communication. Current thinking suggests that several factors contribute to electronic communication gone bad:

- The *lack of nonverbal cues* (e.g., eye contact and other bodily gestures) leaves the communicators without important contextual information used to better evaluate or interpret what is said. Online communications are especially void of emotions which can be lost within these types of communications. Unfortunately, when unknown, people are more apt to assume negative emotions than positive.

- The *anonymity* of the communicator reduces inhibitions (and sometimes appropriateness filters) which leads to more "frank" and uncensored statements and nonexistent consequences.

- *Attempts at humor*, especially sarcasm, may be misinterpreted as hostile communications given the lack of contextual information and understanding of the source or other user.

- As you can see in the previous example, online communications among young people tends to be terse and laden with a new type of shorthand called *leetspeak* (more on that later). Such cryptic and limited data can easily lead to miscommunication and subject to inaccurate assumptions.

Another potential problem with social networking includes being exposed to inappropriate material (and people). Kids can post all types of provocative photos, videos, music, and other content that you would otherwise not allow your child to experience. Adults are doing it too. In fact, "adult entertainers" such as Jenna Jameson are using social networks to promote themselves (see http://www.myspace.com/jennajameson). Here is a cross-section of samples of the types of pages your children could run into:

❏ Playboy Girls of MySpace (http://www.playboy.com/girls/sex/features/girlsofmyspace/)

❏ Entrepreneurs such as Tila Tequila (http://www.myspace.com/tilatequila)

❏ Hillary Scott is a self-proclaimed Anal Princess. (http://tinyurl.com/3cunya)

❏ Mike & Fran WORLD X PRODUCTIONS®, "Reality porn at it's best!" (http://www.myspace.com/WorldXProductions)

❏ Tatiana Stone promotes her "club" (http://www.myspace.com/tatiannastone)

❏ Ashley Lawrence promotes her adult site (http://www.myspace.com/fembomb)

❏ M.A.U.S. (myspacers against underage sluts; http://groups.myspace.com/myspacersagainstunderagesluts)

Educational Media Corporation®, Box 21311, Minneapolis, MN 55421-0311

One of my main concerns with social networking is the way in which it may consume childrens' time and attention at the expense of academic success. It is common for many kids to spend 3-5 hours per day online networking, chatting, posting, etc. This amounts to a half time job! Can you imagine if that kind of time was invested in studying? Or what about a fraction of that time to do chores or have fun with the family?

Social Networking Safeguards

A child wanting an account on one or more social networking sites is getting more difficult to avoid as they increase in popularity. I still say that parents have the tough job of making unpopular decisions which may include that their child does not get to have a MySpace or other social network account. If, however, you do decide to allow this, consider some precautions:

1. Get an account for yourself and learn about the "ins" and "outs" of the system. Find out about the features and capabilities and keep up with changes. Frequent Help and Frequently Asked Question (FAQ) pages such as the one at MySpace (http://www.myspace.com/faq). Also, check out the wonderful online and book resources increasingly available with parents in mind (Visit my site, http://www.GuardingKids.com, for a list).

2. Monitor the amount of time your child spends online, both in front of a computer, cell phone, or any electronic device. No more than 1 hour a day is reasonable.

3. Remind your child that a social network profile and forums are public spaces. Don't post anything you wouldn't want the world to know (e.g., your phone number, address, IM screens name, or specific whereabouts). Avoid posting anything that would make it easy for a stranger to find you, such as where you hang out every day after school. Also, don't post anything that could potentially embarrass you or your loved ones, now or in the future.

4. Make sure your child inputs his or her correct age so that automatic safeguards will kick in. For example, on most social network sites, members under 18 years old are prevented from participating in group discussions on designated mature topics. Additionally, safety tips aimed at young members appear as they browse the site. On MySpace in particular, Profiles belonging to members younger than 16 years old are set by default to only be visible to MySpace members on their friends list. Their information, photos, and the ability to contact them are only available to members they know. Adults are blocked from contacting members under 16 unless they know the younger member's last name or e-mail address. [45]

5. Make sure that your child's account has privacy settings turned on. This doesn't make one's account invisible although much of the content is concealed.

6. If you feel it necessary, you may want to subscribe to a monitoring service such as http://www.myspacewatch.com/.

Cyberbullying

One of the worst ways that some children use online communication tools is to hurt other children in a process now known as cyberbullying. Cyberbullying involves the use of information and communication technologies such as e-mail, cell phone, text messaging, instant messaging, defamatory personal Websites, and defamatory online personal polling websites, to support deliberate, repeated, and hostile behavior by an individual or group, that is intended to harm others." [46] It seems to be even worse than live bullying because the perpetrators are not bound my time or space, and the audience can also be much, much bigger. With the power of technology, the offenses can be significantly more cruel because they can incorporate a rich array of media (sounds, altered graphics, text, video, slide shows, and photos) when delivering the attacks.

Consider the following real situations among cyberbullying victims as reported in one national newspaper: [47]

- When Joanne had a row with a longtime friend last year, she had no idea it would spill into cyberspace. But what started as a spat at a teenage sleep over swiftly escalated into a three-month harangue of threatening e-mails and defacement of her web log. "It was a non-stop nightmare," says Joanne, 14, a freshman at a private high school in Southern California. "I dreaded going on my computer."

- Ashlee, a former elementary school teacher in Birmingham, Ala., says she was "sickened" by the manner girls manipulated one another with instant messages. "I grew to hate that," she said.

- "If I find you, I will beat you up," one message read. Frightened, Michael blocked their IM addresses but didn't tell his parents for two weeks. "It scared me," he recalls. "It was the first time I was bullied."

- At one Elementary School in Fairfax, Va. last year, sixth-grade students conducted an online poll to determine the ugliest classmate, school officials say.

- Cyberbullying is so pervasive in one New York county that officials held a half-day conference last month for students, parents, teachers and law-enforcement officials. Six hundred attended.

- "The person was pretending it was me, and using it to call people names," the 14-year-old Seattle student said. "I never found out who it was."

In a startling case that occurred in June 2003 a twelve-year-old Japanese girl killed her classmate because she was angry about messages that had been posted about her on the Internet. In another example, Canadian teenager David Knight's life became hell when a group of his school mates established a "Hate David Knight" website and posted denigrating pictures and abuse and invited the global community to join in the hate campaign.[48] In another case, a boy named Jeff was the target of relentless bullying. The perpetrators used the computer to launch attacks at Jeff and even destroyed a video game he and his friend worked on all summer. Jeff committed suicide by hanging after two years of persistent harassment. [49] These are only a few examples of this significant and growing problem among children (Studies about the frequency of cyberbullying suggest that cyberbullying is affecting a significant minority of school-age children, with nearly 25 to 35 percent of respondents claiming to have been bullied in chat rooms, e-mail, and via text messages.)

Researchers across various disciplines have collected a rich array of examples of how high-tech bullying takes place which highlights the complexity of the problem:

- **Exclusion**: Exclusion is the process of designating who is a member of the "in-group" and who is an "outcast." In some cases, this is done by who has a mobile phone and who has not. Students, particularly girls, will also omit certain other girls from e-mail lists, chat room conversations and so on. [50] Sometimes, the victim of exclusion is unaware that she has become a target of exclusion. She comes to school and realizes that the day is different. Others avoid making eye contact with her. People will not sit next to her during lunch, walk with her down the hall, or greet her. Why does this happen? Some girls use this form of cyberbullying because they are just plain mean. Others are fearful that if they do include the target, they will be the next target for exclusion.

- **Flaming**: Flaming is a heated argument, frequently including offensive or vulgar language, that occur in online communication environments, such as discussion boards or groups, chat, or newsgroups. The motive for flaming is often to claim authority or establish a position of superiority. Occasionally, flamers wish to upset and offend other members of a forum, in which case they are "trolls." Most often however, flames are angry or insulting messages transmitted by people who have strong feelings about a subject. Some consider flaming to be a great way to let off steam, though the receiving party may be less than pleased. [51]

- **Outing**: This includes the public display, posting, or forwarding of personal communication or images, especially communication that contains sensitive personal information or images that are sexual in nature. Increasingly, images taken using mobile phone cameras and mobile phone text messages are used as part of "outing" type bullying. Reading the saved text messages on other's phones can also be part of the outing process. [52] One of the most hurtful ways to "out" someone is when you publicize that a target is homosexual, whether it is true or not.

- **Cyberstalking**: Includes threats of harm, intimidation and/or offensive comments which are sent through personal communication channels. Frequently with cyberstalking there is a threat, or at least a belief, that the virtual could become real stalking. [53] The National Center for Victims of Crime (NCVC) defines cyberstalking as "... threatening behavior or unwanted advances directed at another using the Internet and other forms of online and computer communications." Also, according to the NCVC, cyberstalkers target their victims through chat rooms, message boards, discussion forums, and e-mail. Cyberstalking takes many forms such as: threatening or obscene e-mail; spamming (in which a stalker sends a victim a multitude of junk e-mail); live chat harassment or flaming (online verbal abuse); leaving improper messages on message boards or in guest books; sending electronic viruses; sending unsolicited e-mail; tracing another person's computer and Internet activity, and electronic identity theft.

- **E-mail**: One student sends a threatening or abusive e-mail to another and may even blind copy the e-mail to additional people; [54]

- **Harassment**: Sending hurtful messages (e-mail, text, VOIP, IM, or other form of electronic communication) to someone in a severe, persistent, or pervasive manner.

- **Instant Messaging (IM)**: Several students log on to an IM platform (e.g., America Online's Instant Messenger) and simultaneously "slam" another; [55]

- **Websites**: Some cyberbullies set up derogatory websites or blogs dedicated to one or more victims such as other children, teachers, or administrators.

- **Impersonation**: In yet other cases, students may impersonate someone who they pick as their target while they are online. Then, pretending to be their target, the cyberbully does things such as makes unpopular online comments, sets up offensive websites, flames others – all with the intention of drawing negative attention to the target being impersonated. The result is that the child being impersonated may then become an ongoing target among other cyberbullies or get into trouble at school.

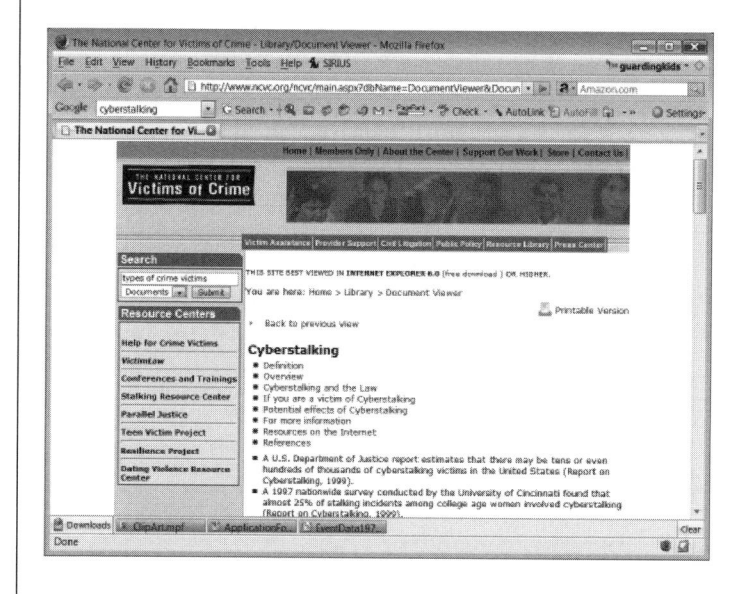

- **Voting/Polling Booths**: Some websites offer users the opportunity to create online polling/voting booths, many at no cost. Cyberbullies can use these Websites to create web pages that allow others to vote online for "The Ugliest, Fattest, Dumbest etc. Boy/Girl" at their respective schools.

- **Hostile Takeover**: When a student learns the password for another student's e-mail, website, or computer account, he or she may use that knowledge to takeover the account. Once she gains access, the student can change the password so that the real owner can no longer access the account. And, the perpetrator may even use the account against the victim. For example, the cyberbully may use the victim's own website to defame, libel, or otherwise harm him. In other cases, the cyberbully may access the victim's account and delete it. For a student that has worked long and hard on a software program, website, or other project and does not have a backup, this really hurts. In a different example, what if a student accesses another student's e-mail account and uses it to cyberbully others. It may be very difficult or even impossible to prove that "it wasn't me."

Again, children seem to view the real world and the online or virtual world on a seamless continuum. Conversations with friends may begin at school and pick up again, on a child's computer, after dinner. Unfortunately, this is also true of cyberbullying behaviors. What begins as a flame war in an Instant Messaging conversation can carry over to the lunch room the next day and include many of the same group members participating in the electronic conversation the night before. More often than not, cyberbullying starts with an incident in the real world and spills over into cyberspace where it is easier and safer to fight others.

What to do if you suspect cyberbullying?

You may notice that your child is acting a bit odd and wonder what is going on with him or her. Know first of all that pre-adolescence and especially adolescence (the teenager years) can be a weird time for everyone even under "normal" circumstances. Still, you may notice a deviation from what you are used to or perhaps extreme changes, especially one or more of the following: [56]

- Your child is using their computer late at night more than usual.

- Your child's grades are declining.

- He or she is misbehaving in school more than usual.

- Changes in ordinary daily activities and conditions such as eating, sleeping, mood swings, etc.

- Your child appears upset after Internet use. Or, in general seems more anxious and fearful, especially as it relates to school.

- There is some evidence that your child is covering their online tracks.

If your child is being cyberbullied:

- Don't freak out. Stay calm and maintain open communication with your child. Let them know that you trust and support them.

- Don't blame the victim. This is not the time for "I told you so" or "You should have" kinds of conversations (actually, it's never a good time for this type of blaming the victim communication, it really doesn't help).

- If they are being bullied and involved in cyberbullying, explain that taking vengeance will not help solve the problem and that it could make the situation worse.

- Work with your child to report the cyberbullying to a trusted adult at school such as a teacher, principal, or counselor.

- Help your child to keep all records including chat transcripts, photos, website pages, e-mails (including full headers) as evidence for future use.

- Inform the perpetrator's Internet Service Provider (ISP) or cell phone service provider of the abuse.

- If you can communicate to the perpetrators and their parents, explain to them that what they are doing is cyberbullying and that you will report to the authorities if it continues. Some kids may not recognize what they are doing as bullying and may believe that it is innocent kids play. Using the word "bullying" can serve as a wake up call.

For a much more in depth discussion of cyberbullying, be sure to check out a book entitled *Cyberbullying and Cyberthreats: Responding to the challenge of online social aggression, threats, and distress* by Nancy E. Willard. [57] What stands out most in this book is Willard's comprehensive coverage, illustrative examples, recommendations for practice, and practical resources. When you get a chance, I recommend you check out the author's website, The Center for Safe and Responsible Internet Use (http://www.csriu.org/), which provides research and outreach services to address issues of the safe and responsible use of the Internet. This site provides guidance to parents, educators, librarians, policy-makers, and others regarding effective strategies to assist young people in gaining the knowledge, skills, motivation, and self-control to use the Internet and other information technologies in a safe and responsible manner.

Unanticipated Effects of Online Communication

When children disclose personal information or voice their (sometimes controversial) opinions, they may also jeopardize themselves or others in yet another way. You see, most everything posted on any website today may possibly, and probably be accessible for all of time. Information shared with others via listserv, websites, IM, blogs, social networks, and other media is typically stored in massive databases, indexed, and easily retrievable for future reference. You or your child may believe that what you communicate today is "no big deal" although, tomorrow, could be seen as ammunition by others to use against you or your loved ones. Adults are already learning this the hard way. A few adult bloggers, for instance, have been fired for writing about their work on personal online journals. According to Krysten Crawford, a CNN/Money magazine reporter, one fellow, for example, landed a dream job with Google Inc. in January of 2005. He was fired less than a month later. His infraction? He ran a blog, where he freely gabbed about his impressions of life at the Mountain View, California based Internet search giant. [58]

A person need not even write about their job to get fired. Ellen Simonetti, also known as "Queen of Sky," is a former flight attendant working for a major airline who was fired from her job in October of 2004 for posting "inappropriate" pictures in uniform on her blog. She was never told which pictures were "inappropriate." You can see the photos for yourself at http://queenofsky.journalspace.com/. One man, Danny Cervantes, used the social network service MySpace.com to create his own profile, where he blogged details about his life as a professional boxer in Ventura, California. The blogs would also drift into other topics, including dilemmas with girls and the latest hangouts. He also used his page to showcase his graphic artwork and pictures of his friends. According to Marjorie Hernandez, who wrote an article circulated by the Scripps Howard News Service, Cervantes was let go from his part-time job as a trainer at La Colonia Boxing Club after the city received an anonymous letter from a parent complaining about the contents of the Website. In the letter, the parent complained about "crude" pictures of Cervantes with women and "X-rated" conversations, Cervantes said.

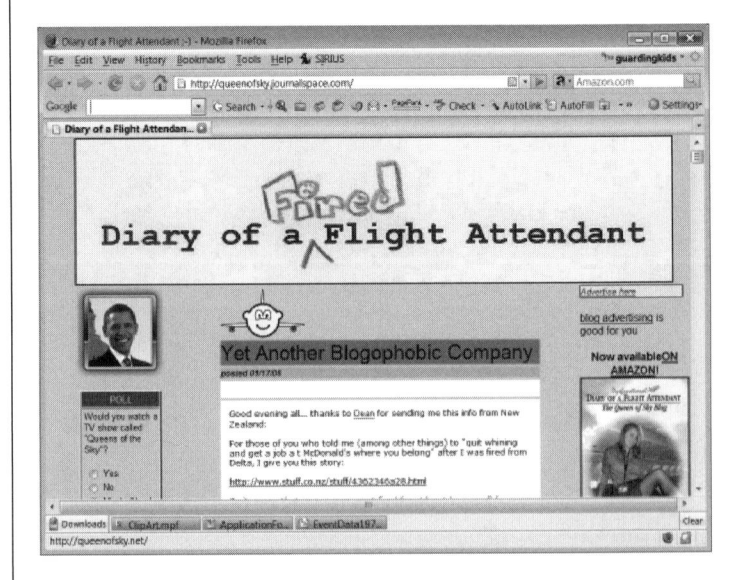

Getting terminated from one's job because of an online posting has become a persistent issue. In fact, one blogger, Heather B. Armstrong, coined a phrase for it in 2002 – "dooced." Heather was fired from her Web design job for writing about work and colleagues on her blog, Dooce.com. The term is now included in one online Urban Dictionary (see http://www.urbandictionary.com/define.php?term=dooced).

Another vivid example of blogging fallout is how Maya Marcel-Keyes, daughter of conservative politician Alan Keyes, posted personal details about her life including the fact that she is a lesbian. This information became an issue during her father's run for a U.S. Senate seat in Illinois after he made anti-gay statements during his campaign.

These are only a few of many examples of how a personal communication can become a public drama, more is sure to come. Certainly, blogs may be consumed by an unintended audience such as potential employers, romantic partners, or curious reporters who may later use your online musings against you in ways that you could not have imagined.

Cell Phones

Today's cell phones are more than just phones, they are high-tech gadgets that also serve as a mini-computers. Today's cell phones allow users to surf the web, conduct text chats with others, take photos, record video, download and listen to music, play games, update blogs, send instant text messages, keep a calendar and to-do list, and much more. For children and teenagers, they allow for anytime, anywhere communication especially with friends. With cell phones, children are always only a few buttons away, highly connected and instantaneously available. Parents who allow their children to have cell phones feel secure that they too can contact their sons and daughters at a moment's notice.

Many parents also feel relieved to know that their children have easy access to them and to emergency personnel if needed. For instance, a cell phone is especially convenient for kids who participate in after school activities such as sports or clubs. If the activity ends early or late, or has been canceled, kids can call their parents to let them know about the changes. Kids can also call their parents to ask for permission should last-minute changes in their plans occur. Some parents even use their children's cell phones as tracking devices that allow them to identify their child's location at any time which would certainly come in handy in the event of a kidnapping or lost child.[59] From a parent's perspective, these are all good reasons to supply our children with cell phones. However, the convenience that cell phones offer us must be judged against the hazards they pose to all people and especially the cell phone user. The remainder of this chapter reviews the downsides of child cell phone use and provides recommendations for parents to consider.

Text Messaging

When a voice conversation is overkill, too embarrassing (such as in, I don't want to say "Hi Mom" in front of my friends), or just not convenient, text messaging (also known as texting) really comes in handy. Texting is the "killer app[60]" these days which has eclipsed e-mail communication now considered among kids as "old school." Even many parents admit that it is one of the best ways to check up on their kids, remind them of important events, or quickly communicate a change in plans. So what do parents, educators, and other care takers need to know about the potential risks with text messages?

First, texting is a primary method for communicating harassment or intimidation as part of an overall cyberbullying strategy. For instance, some estimate that more than one in every eight children has been bullied by e-mail or text message.[61] Some do it directly although others are more creative. For example, a child will borrow another child's cell phone (this child is actually the target of cyberbullying) and then use that phone to cyberbully a third student. The receiver of the text messages may then retaliate against the student who owns the cell phone, just as the first student planned. Another way that devious kids cyberbully by texting is that they will borrow their victims phone to text their own cell phone. The text message comes with the targets phone number which is now used to launch a relentless barrage of text message attacks from one or more other students.

Another problem is that texting may give predators a secret path to kids. The same cell phones that parents buy as safety devices for their children are the gadgets that pedophiles and predators use to "prep" kids for sexual encounters. One television station reported, for example, on a second-grader who was solicited by a 31 year old man on his cell phone. The child did respond to the text messages and an exchange of messages followed, including the man's request of the child's name, age and address.[62] In another case, a 26-year-old P.E. teacher admitted to having sex with a 14-year-old student in the school's parking lot. Detectives from the town's police department said they found nude pictures of the teacher on the teen's cell phone along with text messages.[63] Some still remember when Florida law enforcement officials investigated former Republican Rep. Mark Foley, whose e-mails and instant messages to teenage former congressional pages shocked the country. These are just a few examples of many ... it does happen.

Have you heard of text-related injuries? The problem stems from logging in lots of miles on those tiny cell phone keypads. Literally, hundreds of billions of text messges are sent from around the world every year. One girl, Morgan Pozgar, entered a text messaging competition and said that she trained by sending on average 8,000 text messages a month to her friends – an astonishing rate of one every five and a half minutes.[64] You see, to text, people tend to hold cell phones in their fingers and press the tiny keys with their thumbs. This reverses the computer keyboard position, where clumsy thumbs are relegated to the space bar and let fingers do the typing. This can lead to Repetitive Stress Syndrom (RSI), the symptoms of which include pain and immobility in the joints, nerves and muscles from the fingers to the neck. RSI is caused by repetitive movements and fatigue resulting from natural stresses and strains on the body.[65]

Although controversial, yet another possible risk of text messaging is how it may contribute to increasingly poor spelling and writing skills in youth. Because texting uses intentionally misspelled words, nonstandard abbreviations, letter substitutions, and little or no punctuation, some educators believe that it encourages poor literacy and a blunt, choppy style at odds with academic rigor. Yet, others say that texting is simply a new form of literacy. This all remains to be seen.[66]

Cell Phone Distractions

"Driving While Dialing." In November of 2005 a Highlands Ranch, Colorado 17-year-old allegedly lost control of his car while text-messaging and hit a bicyclist who died two days after the accident. The boy was charged with a misdemeanor which comes with a maximum sentence of one year in prison.

The fact that cell phones pose a great risk when combined with driving cannot be of any surprise to anyone. Let's face it. First, drivers must take their eyes off the road while dialing. Second, people can become so absorbed in their conversations or other cell phone use that their ability to concentrate on the act of driving is severely impaired, jeopardizing the safety of vehicle occupants and pedestrians alike. In fact, the National Highway Transportation Safety Association has determined that driver inattention is a primary or contributing factor in as many as 25 percent of all police-reported traffic accidents.[67] It's not just talking and text messaging, the two most popular cell phone applications. Remember, cell phones have – and will continue to expand their capabilities as a central communication/collaboration device which already includes access to the World Wide Web, global positioning system (GPS) navigation, camera, voice memo recorder, productivity tools, e-mail clients, and much more. Already available is the ability to watch live television on your cell phone through cell phone service providers and other companies such as mobitv (http://www.mobitv.com/). So, in addition to drinking and driving, parents ought to seriously consider a rule for their children that includes no cell phone use and driving.

Time Away from Homework. Technology affords teens (and adults) a host of ways to do something other than what they are supposed to such as homework. In the adult world, it is a common experience that the lines between work and leisure have been blurred. Adults often work at home and play at work – e-mailing and text messaging friends and family, passing along jokes and family photos, shopping, viewing pornography, reading the news, and even gambling. Business owners are increasingly relying on stealth spying programs to snoop on their employees to make sure that their activities are both appropriate and work related. Their bottom lines are at stake. As parents, we too have the responsibility to help our children focus on their productivity. Their "bottom lines" are academic achievement and success.

Socializing on the phone while trying to do homework or study, no matter what your teen says, is not optimal. Realize too that you may not even hear a child talking on the phone and assume that the silence emanating from their rooms is the sound of a diligent student being productive. Realize, however, that children can use their cell phones for a variety of purposes that goes beyond talking such as updating their online blog (e.g., see Nokia Lifeblog which automatically builds your diary as you take photos and videos, and send and receive messages; see http://europe.nokia.com/nokia/0,,71742,00.html), text messaging, or posting photos to their social network spaces such as MySpace.

Mounting Minutes

Since consumers must be 18 in order to purchase a cell phone contract in the United States, most parents are buying the phones their children carry. This is good news because parents can choose a plan that fits how the cell phone will be used and can review monthly cell phone bills which typically includes a log itemizing phone activity. However, problems still exist. For one, children can quickly go over their allotted minutes which can leave their parents with bills that can easily approach hundreds of dollars for the month. One thing that helps is the availability of cell phone plans that include unlimited minutes during certain hours or between certain cell phone carriers.

Choosing a plan with unlimited minutes can ease the risk of mounting monthly phone charges although does not solve the problem of understanding what kids do with those unlimited minutes. For instance, cell phone features such as text messaging and Web browsing are increasingly included in bundles with extra weekend and night minutes, in essence, giving children unlimited and unsupervised access to each other and to the Internet. Thus, parents who have a supervision system that works for computers at home may unknowingly give their children a work-around for getting into trouble outside of the home in a way that is even more convenient to the child.

Cell Phones and Gaming

According to MSNBC technology correspondent Bob Sullivan, when cellular phone games were simple, such as the knock offs of the Atari-era "Breakout," there wasn't much to worry about. [68] But newer phones with color displays and higher processing power create a landscape that might make some parents worried about what type of games their kids are playing on the bus home from school. Games and videos with sex and violence are now a technological possibility — even if the screens are still small, and the characters pixilated. And then there's the more subtle messages sent by some games as shown in this cell phone game's description:

"Prince of Persia," by Gameloft, urges players to rescue a kidnapped harem of women. "The Sultan's wives have been kidnapped by the Vizier in order to carry out experiments on abstinence. The Sultan's real mad! He no longer knows how to express his desires. Seven female prisoners – and only you can set them free and bring them back to life!"

Complicating matters further is the fact that game ratings can't be used on cell phones — the technology does not currently allow it. Console and computer games have ratings on the outside of the package, so parents at least know what they are getting into when they make a purchase. Since cell phone downloads offer no method for displaying ratings before purchase, there is no way to enforce a rating system. To be fair, cell phone companies seem to be doing a pretty good job of regulating themselves and preventing putting inappropriate games in the hands of children via their cell phones. How long, however, can they resist this incredibly lucrative market? When will profit grease the slippery slope of providing increasingly more violent and sexually charged games? Even now, cell phone games have changed from old style and innocuous arcade games such as Tetris to games with more elaborate (and questionable) plots. For instance, one cell phone game is described as the following:

Play as Tanner, undercover cop and action hero, and bring down a car theft ring on the city streets of Miami, Istanbul and Nice. DRIV3R is packed with driving and out-of-car missions that keep the action fresh and exciting, including chases, timed racing, combat and much more! DRIV3R's explosive action and incredible depth will keep your pulse racing in high gear!

Another cell phone game, Tom Clancy's Rainbow Six® 3, for example, may entice children with the following description:

You lead your team on missions to the four corners of the world. Once you've survived the terrorists' ambush in a snowbound Swiss village, you'll have to flush them out of a luxurious villa in Curaçao and confront them in a Venezuelan commercial port. Tactics and action are at the heart of the explosive mixture found in Rainbow Six® 3. You'll have to make the right decisions at the right time if you want to stay alive and save the hostages in a cowardly kidnap plot. With the intuitive interface, it's easy to position your team and launch a deadly surprise attack! Choose from a range of orders to give your squad to neutralize the terrorist threat: throw flashbang or frag grenades, secure a position, defuse bombs or eliminate enemy snipers using an original game mode, and more! But beware, your enemies are highly trained and lethal traps are waiting you.[69]

This game is fashioned after the PC version of the same title, which, incidentally, is rated "M" for mature.

Public Nuisance

Eighty-seven percent of Americans in a 2006 ABC News "20/20" survey say they encounter cell phone gabbing at least sometimes, and a majority – 57 percent – hear it often. Among the people who see it, nearly six in 10 say it bothers them "a lot." [70] I would bet that the numbers are even higher today. Private conversations have gone public which most people would agree are, at best, annoying. We've all been subjected to mundane and grating conversations which start with questions like, "Where are you?" and "What you're doing?" We can now add to the mix teen conversations about dating, parental feuds, "he said, she said," and what everyone is "up to." Could it be that teens whom have grown accustomed to anytime, anywhere communication may contribute to this seemingly growing problem? And if so, then how can we be critical since youngsters are only doing what adults are now doing in droves? ... we talk in our cars, in buses, malls, offices – that is, everywhere and anywhere without much regard for our public surroundings.

I agree with Dan Briody of Infoworld when he says that there comes a time in any technological revolution when some basic guidelines need to be laid down. It happened when e-mail exploded on the scene and people started to learn some basic do's and don'ts around the new medium. There are some real abuses of wireless technology being perpetrated all around us, and the time has come to create some social order out of the cell phone chaos. [71] Here are a few must see websites about appropriate cell phone use in public:

- The Ten Commandments of cell phone etiquette. http://tinyurl.com/7wjfv or http://tinyurl.com/3b4o9w if you like to see them in pictures.
- Teaching Kids Cell Phone Etiquette By Jan Faull, MEd. http://tinyurl.com/2re2sa
- A MediaWise® Parent Guide: Cell Phones and Your Kids (PDF) http://www.mediafamily.org/network_pdf/cellphon_guide.pdf
- Children, Mobile Phones and the Internet: the Mobile Internet and Children. http://www.childnet-int.org/downloads/tokyo-conference.pdf
- Various articles about kids and cell phone use from KidsWireless.com. http://www.kidswireless.com/articles/

Cell Phones and Pornography

Cell-phone pornography (also known as mobile pornography or mo-po for short) is a fast-growing business that analysts expect will generate about $2 billion in global revenue by 2009. Already, U.S. sales of erotica or porn distributed via cell phones were estimated at about $30 million in 2005. [72] The least restrictive website I found on the Internet (which I won't mention lest I advertise for them) provides visitor with a warning:

"If you are under 18 years of age, or if it is illegal to view adult material in your community, please do not click this link. [Okay, whether you're a kid or adult ... is this not an invitation to click?] We can't be held responsible for your actions. We are not acting in any way to send you this information; you are choosing to received (sic) it! Continuing further means that you understand and accept responsibility for your own actions, thus releasing the creators of this web page and our service provider from all liability. All persons depicted herein were at least 18 years of age at the time of the photography."

That's it. No other means of age verification. All the child has to do is agree to the terms of condition:

YOU HEREBY ACKNOWLEDGE AND REPRESENT THAT YOU KNOW AND UNDERSTAND THAT THE MATERIALS PRESENTED AT, AND/OR DOWNLOADABLE FROM, THE WEBSITE INCLUDE EXPLICIT VISUAL, AUDIO, AND/OR TEXTUAL DEPICTIONS OF NUDITY AND SEXUAL ACTIVITIES, INCLUDING WITHOUT LIMITATION, HETEROSEXUAL, BI-SEXUAL, HOMOSEXUAL, AND TRANSSEXUAL ACTIVITIES OF AN EXPLICIT SEXUAL NATURE; THAT YOU ARE FAMILIAR WITH MATERIALS OF THIS KIND; THAT YOU ARE NOT OFFENDED BY SUCH MATERIALS; AND THAT BY AGREEING TO THESE TERMS AND CONDITIONS YOU ARE WARRANTING TO THE COMPANY THAT

YOU ARE INTENTIONALLY AND KNOWINGLY SEEKING ACCESS TO SUCH EXPLICIT SEXUAL MATERIALS FOR YOUR OWN PERSONAL VIEWING. BY CREATING A FREE ACCOUNT, YOU HEARBY (sic) AGREE TO RECEIVE FREE VIDEO OFFERS VIA E-mail. TO STAY ON OUR E-MAIL LIST, THERE IS NO NEED TO DO ANYTHING. IF YOU DO NOT WISH TO BE CONTACTED BY US VIA E-MAIL, PLEASE CLICK ON THE UNSUBSCRIBE LINK LOCATED IN THE FOOTER OF THE E-MAIL AND YOU WILL BE REMOVED FROM OUR LIST. YOU HEREBY FURTHER AFFIRM AND WARRANT THAT YOU ARE CURRENTLY OVER THE AGE OF EIGHTEEN (18) YEARS (TWENTYONE (21) IN PLACES WHERE EIGHTEEN (18) YEARS IS NOT THE AGE OF MAJORITY) AND ARE CAPABLE OF LAWFULLY ENTERING INTO AND EXECUTING THE TERMS OF THIS AGREEMENT.

Actually, this text only comes up if the visitor clicks on the appropriate link. A visitor could simply just check off that he or she has read these terms without ever really reading them. Notice that according to the terms, the user also agrees to receive video offers via e-mail which, my guess is, will be pornographic in nature and difficult to stop.

Basically, anyone with a cell phone can automatically download a new porn video clip every day for free.

Video Recording Trouble

Indeed, cell phones (and other handheld devices) have become the Swiss Army Knives of the digital generation. They let users do everything from take digital photos and listen to music to play games and surf the Web. And now, better than ever before, shoot video. While the quality of the video doesn't come close to what a regular digital video recorder can do, cell phones allow users to record short, anytime, anywhere video clips that can be sent instantly to others as a video phone message or an e-mail attachment. As long as you have your phone with you, you are ready to capture tomorrow's "Funniest Home Video" or segment on Real TV. Video clips can also quite easily be posted on the Web, for free, and sometimes for sale. For instance, on TextAmerica.com (a mobile blog or moblog), you can find numerous video clips, usually 10 to 15 seconds in length, showing jerky video snapshots of everything from ordinary life to the bizzare caught on tape. Hundreds of these types of places where kids (and others) can post their work exist. One of the most well known, Google Video and YouTube (these are integrated), maintains an "open online video marketplace, where you can search for, watch and even buy an ever-growing collection of TV shows, movies, music videos, documentaries, personal productions and more." They take all kinds of videos (after it passes an unpublished approval process), including those created via cell phone.

For the most part, I suspect that our children, use photo and video capabilities of cell phones to temporarily capture fun, silly, impromptu moments. Other quick thinking kids may even capture news in the making, sometimes incidents in which they are involved. One kid, for example, recorded his bus driver's profanity-laced tirade during an uproar on a school bus which later found its way on national news. Some kids may think it funny to use their cell phones to capture inappropriate images or video. Because cell phones have become so small and indiscreet, they can be used without great risk of detection. For instance, you may have heard of *upskirting* or *downblousing*. These terms are used to describe how some people take secret pictures or video of others, in various states of undress, or under their dress, with their camera phones (and then often times uploading the pictures or video to the Internet). Put the term "upskirt" in any photo or video hosting service and you'll see what I mean (e.g., try http://www.flickr.com/search/?q=upskirt or http://video.google.com/videosearch?q=upskirt&hl=en). One kid was arrested after he and another high school student videoed themselves in a sex act on one of their camera phones, and the boy shared it with his friends. Copies of the video found their way to many of the adult shops in the community, and from there someone got the bright idea to put it online for auction. [73]

Win-Win Cell Phone Solutions

How can parents enjoy the benefits of staying connected with their children while also diminishing the risks that arise when cell phones and children mix? Well, for one, I hope that you have gotten the message throughout this book that, as a parent or care taker, it is important to stay focused, be assertive, and maintain your ground. It may very well be that the answer to owning a personal cell phone is simply, "No." You may determine that in the event of an emergency, your child will already have enough access to you and to emergency personnel by virtue of all the communication possibilities around them. In stores, malls, schools, etc., there are plenty of ways to immediately communicate. I'm sure you have noticed that no matter what the emergency (e.g., school crisis, car accident, etc.), the level of response for school and emergency personnel is amazing. Helpers (and the media) are on the scene within minutes. You will be notified or become aware of any problems very quickly. In special circumstances such as going out to a party, football game, or field trip, your child can always just borrow yours for a day or two.

If you decide that, for whatever reason, your child should have a cell phone handy, you might consider getting one that is programmable and includes parental controls. This means that you can program the phone to only accept certain calls from you and your family members, for instance. And, these phones typically have presets for ambulance, fire, and police. Finally, many of these phones designed for children include GPS locator services. Here are a few examples:

- ChitterChatter Kids Phone (http://www.hop-on.com/kidsphone.html)
- The TicTalk™ Mobile Phone (http://www.mytictalk.com/Leapfrog/)
- Firefly Mobile (http://www.fireflymobile.com/)
- Migo from Verizon Wireless (http://estore.vzwshop.com/search/devices/lg_migo.html)

Chapter 5: Gaming

If you have kids around you – your own kids, grandkids, nieces, nephews, students, or little neighbors – I can safely assume that electronic video games are a part of your life. Like the Internet, they are everywhere. They exist on our desktop computers, laptops, handhelds, cell phones, iPods, and on the web. We also play them on dedicated gaming devices such as a PlayStation, PlayStation Portable (PSP), Gameboy, Xbox, Xbox 360, Sega Genesis, Gamecube, Nintendo 64, and so on. Even these are becoming multifaceted, helping its users to access a fountain of media. For example, in addition to playing games, the PSP allows the user to listen to music, view photos, watch videos, and connect wirelessly to the Internet. Video games are also becoming increasingly realistic. I bet you too have noticed that they are now quite sophisticated, vivid, and realistic in nature – and getting more so every year. In fact, it is known that one of the goals of the electronic video gaming industry is to make video games so realistic that, for example, you will not be able to tell the difference between a live broadcast of a boxing match and one that is being played via a video game console. My estimation is that this goal will be achieved before this decade ends.

Because video games provide realistic experiences that are unattainable and/or inappropriate in the real world, they have become part of a multibillion dollar industry that continues to show great promise for profits. According to the Entertainment Software Association (ESA) 2006 report entitled *Essential Facts About the Computer and Video Game Industry* (see http://www.theesa.com), I shouldn't worry too much about video games and children because:

- 69% of people who play video games are actually head of households;
- The average age of gamers is 33 (Although fully 31% of gamers are under the age of eighteen). It seems as if an entire generation that began gaming as children has kept playing;
- The average age of the most frequent game purchaser is 40;
- Games rated as mature are only a small portion (15%) of the video sold that are rated for teens or for everyone;
- 89% of parents are present with their children during the time video games are purchased;
- 61% of parents believe that video games are a positive part of their children's lives;
- Parents play video games with their children when they are asked to and because they view it as a fun activity for the entire family. They also view game playing as a good opportunity to socialize and supervise their children;
- Gamers devote more than triple the amount of time spent playing games each week to exercising or playing sports, volunteering in the community, religious activities, creative endeavors, cultural activities, and reading (79% of game players of all ages report exercising or playing sports an average of 20 hours a month.)

So, according to the ESA, video games are indeed pervasive although mostly used among adults who are playing games, more often than not, that are rated as appropriate for teenagers or younger. These adults seem to be getting plenty of exercise and do spend some kind of time with their kids. But I'm still concerned. Why? Because there are still millions of children playing video games; because chances are pretty good that many are playing electronic games that are violent and sexual in nature; because there exists some parents who may be role modeling excessive, maybe inappropriate video game playing; and because the jury is still out on the effects of various types of games on child development, behavior, and academic achievement to name a few.

That last sentence, ... *the jury is still out on the effects of various types of games on child development, behavior, and academic achievement,* may have taken you by surprise. When we learn about video games from the popular print, television, and related media, we are led to believe that we are nurturing a new generation of bullies, terrorists, womanizers, and murderers (note that the media typically focuses on violent games and not other more educationally oriented games). Read the research, however, and you'll notice a sense of uncertainty and even misleading conclusions. Some research shows some short-term increases in aggression after playing violent video games, even when controlling for other variables such as levels of pre-existing mental and intellectual conditions. Other research shows no effects. Yet other research on the effects of violent video games are so poorly designed, it doesn't matter what they show, the results are unreliable. The best studies in this area are correlational in nature, not causational. (Note that the extent of research in this area is relatively lacking, probably due to the very difficult nature of controlling for the many human variables that could make a difference in outcomes). What this means is that there seems to be a short term *relationship* or *connection* between playing violent games and increased aggression among players though it is quite uncertain that playing the games *caused* or led to the increased aggression.

Many alternative explanations exist for the connection between playing violent video games and increases in real live aggression. For instance, it could be that a child who is showing increased levels of aggression could be reacting to other factors such as a divorce or death. And it is the increased aggression that actually causes increased video game playing of a violent nature. That is, life events may change levels of aggression which in turn has an affect on our preferences for the types of video games we seek out. It could also be that your gender may play a part in how you are affected by video games. A larger percentage of males tend to play video games deemed as violent as compared to females (about 62% of males versus 38% of females). Also, there is some evidence to suggest that males are more desensitized to interpersonal conflict after exposure to media violence than females. Another explanation may involve personality factors such as temperament which also appears to have a role. People with mental health problems or those viewing media violence under the influence of alcohol or drugs might also be susceptible to violence. Individuals with mental health problems might believe the images they see and, as a result, transpose representations of violent behavior onto themselves, affecting their view of self and others around them.[74]

One court case in particular illuminated the disparity between what the media portrays and what others propose to be the overall truth. The case was described in a *Brief Amici Curiae* of Thirty-three Media Scholars in Interactive Digital Software Association, et al. v. St. Louis County, et al. The summary of the argument goes like this:

Both the St. Louis County Council, in passing Ordinance #20.193, and the district court, in upholding it, relied on the assumption that video games containing "graphic violence" cause violent behavior. The Council heard testimony from psychologist Craig Anderson that playing violent video games "for as short as 10 to 15 minutes" causes "aggressive behavior" and, more broadly, that "there is a causal connection between viewing violent movies and TV programs and violent acts." The trial court relied on these statements, adding that according to Anderson, video games are "addictive" and "provide a complete learning environment for aggression."

Both the County Council and the court were mistaken. Most studies and experiments on video games containing violent content have not found adverse effects. Researchers who do report positive results have generally relied on small statistical differences and used dubious "proxies" for aggression, such as recognizing "aggressive words" on a computer screen. Indeed, research on media violence more generally has also failed to prove that it causes – or is even a "risk factor" for – actual violent behavior. As psychologist Guy Cumberbatch noted:

The real puzzle is that anyone looking at the research evidence in this field could draw any conclusions about the pattern, let alone argue with such confidence and even passion that it demonstrates the harm of violence on television, in film and in video games. While tests of statistical significance are a vital tool of the social sciences, they seem to have been more often used in this field as instruments of torture on the data until it confesses something which could justify publication in a scientific journal. If one conclusion is possible, it is that the jury is not still out. It's never been in. Media violence has been subjected to lynch mob mentality with almost any evidence used to prove guilt. [75]

This torturing of research data on media effects has been driven by a "causal hypothesis" held by some psychologists, that youngsters will imitate fantasy violence. There is some common-sense appeal to this hypothesis. But seemingly common-sense notions do not always turn out to be correct. And researchers' attempts to reduce the myriad effects of art and entertainment to numerical measurements and artificial laboratory experiments are not likely to yield useful insights about the way that viewers actually use popular culture. Likewise, in a field as complex as human aggression, it is questionable whether quantitative studies can ever provide an adequately nuanced description of the interacting influences that cause some people to become violent.

Violent crime rates across the United States have fallen significantly in the past decade, even while fantasy violence in entertainment has increased – and while video games, especially violent ones, have become a staggeringly popular form of entertainment. Youth violence in particular has seen dramatic reductions. This does not mean that youth violence is not a serious problem – or for that matter, that media messages do not have powerful effects. But those effects are much more diverse and difficult to quantify than believers in the causal hypothesis generally acknowledge. And efforts to address real-world violence by censoring entertainment are profoundly misguided. [76]

On the other hand, when looking at the larger body of evidence as a whole as compared to individual studies, there does seem to be some legitimate concern. Dr. Craig A. Anderson, a distinguished professor at Iowa State University's Department of Psychology, has reviewed the last 50 years of research on media violence and aggression and has this to say:

On average there is a clear effect: exposure to media violence (including violent video games) increases subsequent aggression. Some of the few contradictory studies can be explained as being the result of poor methods, others may suffer from a too small sample size. But the main point is that even well conducted studies with appropriate sample sizes will not yield identical results. For this reason, any general statements about a research domain must focus on the pooled results, not on individual studies.[77]

As you can start to see, playing violent video games, especially among children, is a controversial topic on many fronts – political, educational, spiritual, personal, and social. The primary message that I want to convey to parents and other adults who take care of children is this: video games are kind of like breakfast cereal – there are plenty to choose from and some are healthier than others. The whole family can enjoy them and they are an important *part* of an overall sensible and well-balanced lifestyle. Balance and moderation is key. Like all technology, I believe that the benefits and risks of video gaming among children must be ultimately determined by their caretakers and, as a result, have an impact on how they parent. To make the best decision for the children in your care, consider various aspects of video games which I describe in the remainder of this chapter.

Positive Potential of Video Games

Consider the following quote, "*Games are widely used as educational tools, not just for pilots, soldiers and surgeons, but also in schools and businesses ... Games require players to construct hypotheses, solve problems, develop strategies, learn the rules of the in-game world through trial and error. Gamers must also be able to juggle several different tasks, evaluate risks and make quick decisions.... Playing games is, thus, an ideal form of preparation for the workplace of the 21st century, as some forward-thinking firms are already starting to realize.*" [78] There is some evidence that supports this powerful statement. For instance, the National Institute on Media and the Family (see http://www.mediafamily.org/facts/facts_effect.shtml) notes the following benefits of playing video games:

❏ Video game playing introduces children to computer technology;

❏ Games can give practice in following directions;

❏ Some games provide practice in problem solving and logic;

❏ Games can provide practice in use of fine motor and spatial skills;

❏ Games can provide occasions for adult and child to play together;

❏ Players are introduced to information technology;

❏ Some games have therapeutic applications with patients;

❏ Games are entertaining.

One article by the Associated Press quipped that, "All those years on the couch playing Nintendo and PlayStation appear to be paying off for surgeons." The article goes on to explain that researchers found that doctors who spent at least three hours a week playing video games made about 37 percent fewer mistakes in laparoscopic surgery and performed the task 27 percent faster than their counterparts who did not play video games. [79] Similarly, the BBC news reported in May of 2003 that United States scientists have found that regular players of shoot-em-up games have much better visual skills than most of the population. The researchers have shown that gamers were particularly good at spotting details in busy, confusing scenes and could cope with more distractions than average. The two scientists also found that with a little game playing the visual skills of anyone can be improved. [80]

Video Games and Physical Health

Other reports point to the benefits of video game playing as well. One in particular that has gained national attention for its positive impact on physical development is *Dance Dance Revolution* (or DDR). You have undoubtedly seen kids playing DDR in mall arcades, movie theaters lobbies, and now, thanks to the release of the home version, at home and in school. DDR is typically played on a dance pad with four arrow panels: left, down, up, and right. These panels are pressed using the player's feet, in response to arrows that appear on the screen in front of the player. The arrows are synchronized to the general rhythm or beat of a chosen song, and success is dependent on the player's ability to time and position his or her steps accordingly. In Dance Dance Revolution, a player must move his or her feet to a set pattern, stepping in time to the general rhythm or beat of a song. During normal gameplay, arrows scroll upwards from the bottom of the screen and pass over stationary, transparent arrows near the top (referred to as the "guide arrows" or "receptors"). When the scrolling arrows overlap the stationary ones, the player must step on the corresponding arrows on the dance platform. Successfully hitting the arrows in time with the music fills the "Dance Gauge" or life bar while failure to do so drains it.

DDR is often criticized as being rigid and bearing little resemblance to actual dancing. [81] To me, kids playing DDR come off as a bit like someone who is hypnotized and who is having a mild yet rhythmic seizure below the waist. Nonetheless, the game seems to promote various skills and is one solution for fighting child obesity which has captured the interest of schools. (For example, at the start of 2006, DDR games are being phased in as part of a fitness program in West Virginia's 756 state schools). [82]

More recently, the Nintendo Wii (pronounced "we" not "why") gaming console has been hailed as one viable solution to the growing problem of obesity among children. Unlike traditional hand-held video games, where users sit on the couch exercising little more than their thumbs, the Wii features digital sensors that let users virtually play the game. In Wii Sports, a game that comes with the console, users mimic the motions used in sports like bowling, tennis and baseball. In other words, the game may be virtual, but the physical exertion is very real. [83] In fact, one online fitness website, traineo.com, has partnered with Nintendo to develop a Wii Fitness Package (see http://wii.groups.traineo.com/).

Video Games and Learning

What about video games and learning or cognitive development (i.e., the mental acquisition of knowledge through thought, experience, and the senses)? Dr. Patricia Greenfield, a professor at the University of California Los Angeles's Department of Psychology, made several discoveries of how this game generation's cognitive skills differ from previous generations. First, the game generation is more comfortable with visual-spatial skills, mental maps, and seeing the computer as a tool. For instance, game generation children can picture folding a shape in their mind without actually doing it. They are very accustomed to a 3D world. In a separate study, McClurg and Chaille discovered that video games help children with spatial visualization. Children in grades 5, 7, and 9 were tested and it was found that those who played video games were significantly better at mentally rotating and visualizing 3D shapes.[84]

One website, http://www.Games2train.com stands out in the world of learning and training for its Game-Based Learning approach – "the ability to marry the fun of playing a video game or computer game together with all the information needed to accomplish learning or training objectives." On this site, you can get information about numerous video games and a description of how they can benefit. Here is a cross-section of examples:

- **Pain Distraction - Free Dive**. A virtual reality-based, 3D undersea exploration adventure that enables players to virtually swim with sea turtles and tropical fish as they hunt for hidden treasure. The game has been shown to distract children suffering from chronic pain or undergoing painful operations in real life with a calming underwater virtual reality. http://www.breakawaygames.com/

- **Commercial-Off-The-Shelf (COTS) History Games**. There are an increasing number of commercial-off-the-shelf games with more-or-less accurate (depending on the game) pictures of almost all periods of history. These games can be useful in helping students understand the periods involved.

- **Life Simulation - Real Lives 2004**. Simulations that let you experience life as, for example, a peasant farmer in Bangladesh, a factory worker in Brazil, a policeman in Nigeria, a lawyer in the US, or a computer operator in Poland, among others. Lets you chose your character's birthplace, sex, whether they are urban or rural, and their potential abilities. http://www.educationalsimulations.com/products.html

- **Reinforcement - Lightspan "Achieve Now."** Contains a series of game-based reinforcement and practice programs. Lightspan is a pioneer in using reinforcement games, and has very comprehensive data on their programs' effectiveness. http://www.lightspan.com/

- **PeaceMaker**. A video game simulation of the Israeli-Palestinian conflict: a tool that can be used to promote a peaceful resolution among Israelis, Palestinians, and young adults worldwide. http://www.peacemakergame.com/

- **Nutrition - "Feed the Monster."** A simple game to teach kids proper nutrition, sponsored by the National Dairy Council. Created by I-SITE. http://www.nutritionexplorations.org/kids/activities/monster2.asp

Edutainment

The new generation of children has been named the game generation. This game generation is accustomed to a high speed, parallel processing, active, fantasy world. Games have changed the learners' cognitive skills so that the game generation can process a lot of information at the same time. Video games are an excellent learning tool because the computer can adjust its difficulty according to the player's preference or need. Video games also teach deductive reasoning, memory strategies, and eye-hand coordination. Working together with software companies, parents, and educators, video games can facilitate children learning the required content for their level as well as make learning fun and applicable to the game generation children. As a result, educators must be willing to learn how to use educational games as a part of constructivist learning in education.[85]

Some off-the-shelf games such as Sim City or Rollercoaster Tycoon, which contain model economies, are being used in education. By playing them it is possible to understand how such models work, and to deduce what their biases are. (In Sim City, for example, in which the player assumes the role of a city mayor, no amount of spending on health care is ever enough to satisfy patients, and the fastest route to prosperity is to cut taxes.) Such games are not only educational but entertaining (hence the neologism "edutainment") allowing kids to learn valuable skills and knowledge under the disguise of a game. Successful edutainment is discernible by the fact that learning becomes fun and teachers or speakers educate an audience in a manner which is both engaging and entertaining. More than ever before, video games have lifted the standards by which children judge the value of their learning experiences both in front of their televisions and in the classroom. Teachers know this as they sometimes feel pressured to compete with the alluring experiences provided by common video games. As a teacher myself, I can tell you that it sometimes feels as if the only way that students will pay attention is if I provide them with activities that lead to an outer body experience, nothing less. As a parent, like any parent, I want to support video game play among my children that leaves them with increased and relevant knowledge and skills. I want them to, as much as possible, "learn and earn" while still having a good time. So how is this already being accomplished? Here are a few of many examples of what is being used and where to get them:

- Tim Rylands, a British teacher in a primary school near Bristol, recently won an award from Becta, a government education agency, for using computer games in the classroom. By projecting the fantasy world of "Myst", a role-playing game, on to a large screen and prompting his 11-year-old pupils to write descriptions and reactions as he navigates through it, he has achieved striking improvements in their English test scores.[86]

- EduProfix is a computer game based on driving cars. You have to drive through the right answer in addition to get through. Developers meant this game for younger children who aren't able to learn from lists on paper (see http://www.eduprofix.com/).

- The Learning Company® sells education software for preschool through high school (see http://www.learningcompany.com/). Here you will find well-trusted brands such as Reader Rabbit® software, Mavis Beacon® software, ClueFinders® software, Kid Pix® software, Adventure Workshop® software and many more.

GuardingKids.com

- A time-tested favorite, *Storybook Weaver Deluxe* inspires and motivates students to author and illustrate their own multimedia story with an easy-to-use word processor and variety of graphic tools. Story ideas that range from fantasy adventures to personal events to historical fiction, and an extensive array of multicultural images from around the world, make Storybook Weaver Deluxe the perfect tool for a wide range of cross-curricular projects. It's also bilingual, so students can write and hear their story's text read aloud in either English or Spanish (http://tinyurl.com/2km2w5).

- VTech, the creator of the Electronic Learning Products (ELP) Category, is a world leader of age-appropriate learning toys. Since 1976, VTech has been developing high-quality, innovative educational products for children from birth to preteen that deliver "smart play" through the combination of entertaining electronic formats and engaging, age-appropriate content that help children learn while having fun (http://www.vtechkids.com/).

- Wild Earth sends players of all ages on a breathtaking safari through the plains of Africa. Their mission: to explore the wild and capture on film the essence and beauty of the natural world around them. Your photos become an integral part of articles that are created from your own experiences! (http://www.wildearthgame.com/).

- TeAch-nology - The Art and Science of Teaching with Technology® - represents a vision of teaching in a world driven by technology. The organization's mission is to provide services designed to support educators' in effectively incorporating technology in teaching and learning. Their goal is twofold: to provide a reservoir of online resources for educators to access at any time and to provide effective tools for designing instruction that are time and energy saving. (http://www.teach-nology.com/downloads/)

- The Incredible Machine: Even More Contraptions gives players dozens of tools that perform an action: balls that bounce, cats that chase (and don't bounce), pulleys, ropes, generators, and yes, mandrill baboons on conveyer belts, bananas a-dangle in front of them. Then players are given a problem to solve with all of this crazy energy. Here's an example: in one puzzle called "Wood is Good," players must get three balls into a box, make wooden toast, and wood-smoke a hunk of Gouda cheese for a mouse. Among the tools available to accomplish this task are a bike pump and an antigravity pad. And this is one of the easy puzzles. There are 250 gizmos to build here, some designed for single players and some designed for head-to-head puzzling competition. There is also a field where players can design their own Rube Goldberg Machine from scratch. The vast amount of projects and their complexity make this a program with staying power. (http://tinyurl.com/2nhubx).

Video Games as the New "Third Place"

Imagine an entire 3D world online, complete with forests, cities, and seas. Now imagine it populated with others from across the globe who gather in virtual Inns and taverns, gossiping about the most popular guild or comparing notes on the best hunting spots. Imagine yourself in a heated battle for the local castle, live opponents from all over collaborating or competing with you. Imagine a place where you can be the brave hero, the kingdom rogue, or the village sage, developing a reputation for yourself that is known from Peoria to Peking. Now imagine that you could come home from school or work, drop your bookbag on the ground, log in, and enter that world any day, any time, anywhere. Welcome to the world of massively multiplayer online gaming (MMOG or MMO for short). [87]

In his book *The Great Good Place*, sociologist Ray Oldenburg makes the argument that American culture has lost many of its third places – spaces for neither work or home but rather informal social life. "The essential group experience is being replaced by the exaggerated self-consciousness of individuals," Oldenburg argues. "American lifestyles, for all the material acquisition and the seeking after comforts and pleasures, are plagued by boredom, loneliness, alienation." Constance Steinkuehler, in his published paper *The New Third Place: Massively Multiplayer Online Gaming in American Youth Culture*, effectively argues that massively MMOGs do indeed function as one novel form of a new "third place" for informal sociability. [88] Steinkuehler, along with her co-author Dimitri Williams, say that MMOGs function not like solitary dungeon cells, but more like virtual coffee shops or pubs where something called "social bridging" (i.e., broad but weak social networks rather than deep but narrow ones) takes place. "By providing places for social interaction and relationships beyond the workplace and home, MMOGs have the capacity to function much like the hangouts of old," they said. And they take it one step further by suggesting that the lack of real-world hangouts "is what is driving the MMO phenomenon" in the first place.

One of the most popular MMOG is an online game called Runescape (http://www.runescape.com/) . This game has been greeted enthusiastically by experts to promote positive understanding and skills among its players that include friendship and teamwork and problem solving. Also, security measures in Runescape are quite impressive. The site employs many trained staff in helping keep their users safer and enforce their strict rules online. Their users are taught not to share personal information, meet strangers offline and to treat others with respect. Unlike some of the newer gaming sites, their users cannot build profiles or upload and share images. If they find that any of their users have violated their safety rules and terms of service, that user may find themselves permanently banned, or their account frozen for extended periods of time.

Negative Potential of Video Games

What really is the harm in playing video games? So far, we have focused mostly on the effects of playing violent games which I believe can be hurtful when played frequently and over a long period of time. I also believe that highly violent or sexual games such as those that show gruesome and bloody killing can be harmful even in the short term. [89] I am also convinced that the context of violent video games can be harmful. For instance, is the violence unjustified? Are acts of violence rewarded such as in gaining "extra lifes," more power, or better weapons? How are women and children depicted? And, what types of graphics are being presented (e.g., blood, gore, mutilation, torture, etc.). As a summary, the National Institute on Media and the Family (see http://www.mediafamily.org/facts/facts_effect.shtml) suggests the following potential negative effects of inappropriate video games:

- Over-dependence on video games could foster social isolation, as they are often played alone.
- Practicing violent acts may contribute more to aggressive behavior than passive television watching. Studies do find a relationship between violent television watching and behavior.
- Women are often portrayed as weaker characters that are helpless or sexually provocative.
- Game environments are often based on plots of violence, aggression and gender bias.
- Many games only offer an arena of weapons, killings, kicking, stabbing and shooting.
- Playing violent video games may be related to aggressive behavior. [90]
- More often games do not offer action that requires independent thought or creativity.
- Games can confuse reality and fantasy.
- In many violent games, players must become more violent to win. In "1st person" violent video games the player may be more affected because he or she controls the game and experiences the action through the eyes of his or her character.
- Academic achievement may be negatively related to over-all time spent playing video games.

Of course, not all games will adversely affect your child in all the ways listed above. However, some games can have a negative influence in at least one of these ways. These potential problems or risks should serve as a checklist of possibilities to consider. Next, I want to pay special consideration to the issue of violence and desensitization.

Violence and Desensitization

Desensitization is one process that counselors and therapists use to help clients reduce their excessive (and often irrational) fears of things like heights, flying, spiders, snakes, blood, and public speaking. After being "desensitized," the person no longer reacts to the object or condition of fear and instead essentially can ignore it. This process can be very helpful when the condition is an important and necessary part of someone's life. For example, desensitization to distressing sights, sounds, and smells of surgery is necessary for medical students to become effective surgeons. Desensitization to battlefield horrors is necessary for troops to be effective in combat. However, desensitization of children and other civilians to violence may be detrimental for both individuals and society. One of the ways that we can determine the level of desensitization to a certain stimulus or condition is to measure someone's heart rate, perspiration levels, and rate of breathing while they are experiencing the stimulus. That is, a person's level of physiological arousal to a situation can help us determine how sensitive they are to that situation.

Some evidence exists to suggest that as little as twenty minutes of playing a violent video games can cause people to become less physiologically aroused by real violence. This can cause problems. For a child who may be at some level desensitized to violence, they may not have strong negative reactions to violence in the real world which may lower their motivation to help or intervene during a violent incident. Lowered sensitivity to violence may also lower the inhibition for being violent as well. This is one reason why researchers believe that the more we are exposed to violence the more we are apt to behave violently in the real world. What may also be worrisome is how children may be exposed to increasingly higher dosages of violence across many media as they get older. They may start by experiencing violence packages on television with non-threatening cartoon-like figures and the total absence of blood and gore. Then, their violence exposure continues to be more realistic, sophisticated, and vivid.[91]

To combat desensitization, we must limit or prevent high levels of exposure to violence across all media including television, movies, and video games.[92] And when children do view violence, we must role model appropriate reactions as if we were watching it for the first time. This is especially true for boys who seem to show greater tendencies to be aggressive and to seek out higher media violence exposure.

Gaming Addictions

Consider the following cases ... On Aug 9, 2005, Reuters reported that a South Korean man who played computer games for 50 hours almost non-stop died of heart failure minutes after finishing his mammoth session in an Internet café. [93] The report goes further by saying that the 28-year-old man planted himself in front of a computer monitor to play online battle simulation and only left the spot over the next three days to go to the toilet and take brief naps on a makeshift bed. A police officer commented that, "We presume the cause of death was heart failure stemming from exhaustion." In a different case, another boy named James often played video games for five hours a day during his summer break, sometimes even more. He boasts 60 games in his room and three consoles — GameCube, PlayStation 2 and Nintendo 64. When his family drags him out of the house, he pockets his portable Nintendo DS, plus his cellphone for playing "Tetris." [94] Then there's a another boy named Will, when during his high school freshman year, he chose a different approach in dealing with his mother's frustration about his pursuit of a very popular virtual reality online game. He ignored her, as his grades plummeted to straight D's in middle school. Will calculated that the hours he spent playing one character equaled "three months and two weeks." One evening, "My mom got my cable cord ... she pulled it and ripped it out," says Will, still a bit wide-eyed at the memory. Later, his mother knocked down a locked door. "I've learned not to mess with my mom," he said.[95]

For most people, computer use and video game play is integrated into their lives in a balanced manner. For others, time spent on the computer or video game is out of balance, and has displaced work, school, friends, and even family. [96] Video games have been proven to lead to a type of addiction among some users. Counterculturalist Timothy Leary was one of the first to liken computers to LSD, noting the mind-expanding, mesmerizing and ritualistic similarities between the two. In 1998 at Hammersmith Hospital in London, Dr. Paul Grasby performed a study that showed that playing video games triggers the release of dopamine in the brain. During the study dopamine levels doubled in the subjects' brain when they played video games, a level of dopamine equivalent to an injection of amphetamines or Ritalin.[97] Dr. David Walsh, a long-time expert and founder of the National Institute on Media and the Family, reports of some children playing over 43 hours a week of video games. [98]

The principles that lead to gaming addictions are not very different from other types of addictions such as gambling. Similar to casino slot machines, playing video games may be highly sustained, both in frequency and duration, due to the way that the games are programmed and experienced. First of all, like Las Vegas style slots, video games use multiple forms of stimuli including high levels of touch (vibrating gamepads), sight (amazingly realistic and vivid video), and sounds (i.e., sound effects and popular songs) which eventually become associated with rewards. Similar to money, free drinks, and more chances to win at the casino, video games offer its players rewards such as finding hidden areas of the games, getting to advanced levels, earning points, getting on the top player list for others to see, and acquiring badges of achievement. Sometimes, these rewards are easy to earn and can be accomplished in very few attempts. At other times though, the process is difficult and requires extensive practice. Some moves result in "bells and whistles" and other moves don't result to much at all. Sometimes the outcome relies on skill, sometimes chance, and other times a combination of these (do you see why some folks are addicted to playing golf?). The gamer may not be quite sure of how any given maneuver translates into a corresponding result. In behavioral psychology, this is known as a *variable interval or variable ratio schedule of reinforcement.* [99] Similar to gambling, electronic gamers may find themselves continually playing until they get to that next reward which may or may not come. The faster and more intense you play, the better your chances. Meanwhile, watching others play and win can also be reinforcing (this is called social or vicarious reinforcement) and influence how much we play. Given that both casino games and video games can be played with many other people over the Internet, this analogy is even more relevant and powerful today than ever before. [100]

Other Problems with Overindulgent Video Game Playing

Other problems are sometimes associated with playing video games, whether they are violent or not. For instance, when students play for longer than 1 hour per day or, on the average, 7-10 hours per week, they may be sacrificing needed homework and study time which could negatively impact academic performance. Relatedly, there is more to life than video games. Kids may not play outdoors, read, or have fun with family and friends in other ways. Like anything else, video games should be played in moderation. Another potential problem is the effect of excessive play on physical development. Watching a screen for prolonged periods can cause vision and eye problems. Sitting in one place for a long time can cause problems in the bones, joints, and muscles (e.g., carpal tunnel syndrom or repetitive stress injuries). Of course there is the issue of how playing video games contributes to a sedentary lifestyle which leads to children being overweight or even obese (not to mention all the snacks they might eat while they play). Games played on the computer or gaming appliance such as PlayStation or Xbox allow the player to connect with others over the Internet with text, video, or voice. This capability introduces some of the same risks that come with other such connections such as being the target of a sexual predator or, at the very least, being negatively influenced by other peers.

What You Can Do

Research shows that the home is the major place where children and adolescents are playing video games – not so much because of the allure of the game per se, but because they perceive of nothing else *more* alluring. That is, they are feeling bored. This is where you come in. It's important to plan with your family members a healthy balance of diverse activities whether they think the activities are fun or not – help them to give it a try. Help them to get involved with sports, music, the theaters, and other organized community activities. Search your community calendar either online or in the newspaper for upcoming events. Another thing you can do is to teach your child to select appropriate games for his her developmental level and according to your own family values. There are several ways to determine appropriateness:

- Consult the ESRB rating on the front and back cover of the game and as referenced in the next section of this chapter. Having said this, however, know that the rating may not always be a perfect indicator of the content. Some games rated by the video game industry as appropriate for "Everyone" may contain potentially harmful content. Many "Teen" games can also be quite violent. Ratings are judgements to which you may or may not agree.

- Play the game yourself first and watch for red flags such as if the game portrays violence frequently; rewards it; treats it humorously; ignores or downplays non-violent solutions; or omits the realistic consequences of violence.

- Play and enjoy the game with your child; check in as your child moves into deeper levels in the game.

- Conduct an online search for game reviews. There are plenty of websites that are dedicated to helping you learn more about various media before allowing them in your home. For instance, the Dove Foundation encourages and promotes the creation, production, distribution and consumption of wholesome family entertainment (http://www.dove.org/). Also check out MediaWise's Kidscore at http://www.mediafamily.org/kidscore/ which is a ratings system by parents for parents. Go to Google.com and enter the keywords "review video games family" (without the quotes) and you'll see other sites that could also be helpful.

- Network with other parents who you trust and hear about what they think.

- Monitor your child while he or she is playing the game until you are completely confident that all aspects of the game are acceptable.

In addition, here are other tips that could help:

- On certain gaming consoles with certain games, you can "turn off" the blood mode which may reduce the intensity of the game.

- Be aware that most computer games can be altered through the use of downloadable programs called "mods" which are broadly available on the Internet and can change the content of the game. Since players create them, mods are not considered in ESRB ratings. It is important for parents to be aware that some mods can alter a game in ways that may not be appropriate for younger players and may be inconsistent with the ESRB rating.

- Learn about and use parental controls. Some of the newer video game console and handheld hardware devices offer parents the ability to limit what type of content their children can access upon activating built-in parental control features. By activating parent controls, you can ensure that your kids only play games that carry ratings you deem appropriate for them.

- Exercise caution with online-enabled games. Some games let users play with other people on the Internet, but it's important to realize that some of these games contain live chat features or other user-generated content, including character models ("skins"), settings ("maps"), weapons and other content that are not part of the ESRB rating. Online-enabled games carry a warning on the package that reads "Game Experience May Change During Online Play." [101]

- Remember that while a new game will completely consume your kids for a while, the novelty should pass and other pursuits will eventually hold more appeal. (Just make sure you make those other pursuits readily available).

Know the ESRB System of Ratings

According to their website at http://www.esrb.org/, the Entertainment Software Rating Board (ESRB) is a non-profit, self-regulatory body established in 1994 by the Entertainment Software Association (ESA). ESRB independently assigns computer and video game content ratings, enforces industry-adopted advertising guidelines and helps ensure responsible online privacy practices for the interactive entertainment software industry. The Board's mission is to provide consumers, especially parents, with accurate and objective information about the age suitability and content of computer and video games so they can make informed purchase decisions.

The rating system includes two parts which includes both a rating category to suggest age-appropriateness, as well as content descriptors to indicate what content may have triggered the rating and/or may be of interest or concern to the consumer. You've seen these ratings everywhere although you may not have paid much attention to what each rating represents before.

Go directly to the Game Ratings & Descriptor Guide by visiting the ESRB website at http://www.esrb.org/ratings/ratings_guide.jsp

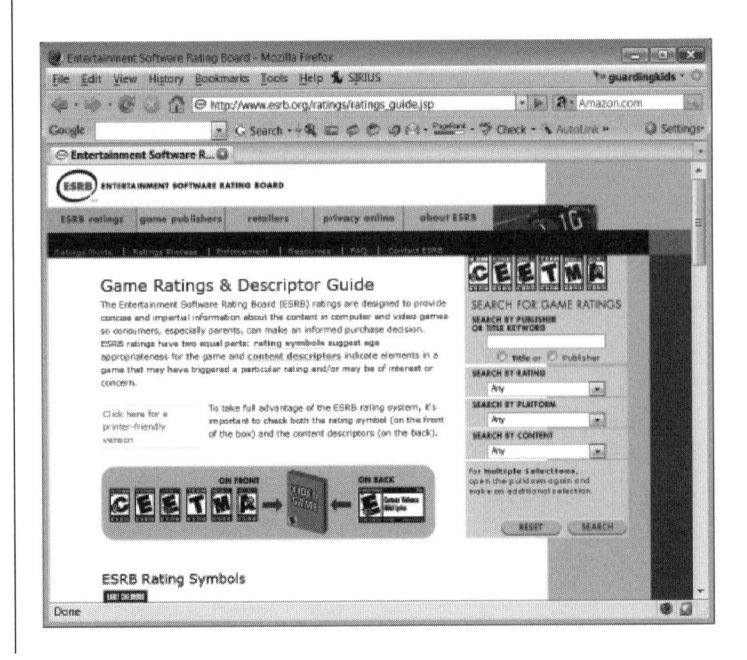

The future of video games promises even greater changes, some will be good and others not so good. Games consoles, computers, and other technologies will become even more powerful and will introduce unprecedented levels of performance. This will, for example, make possible characters with convincing facial expressions, opening the way to games with the emotional charge of films, which could have broader appeal and convince skeptics that gaming has finally come of age as a mainstream form of entertainment. But, to the dismay of many, such advancements will also make depictions of inappropriate behavior even more lifelike.

Yet, one thing stands for sure, video games are not going away. Perhaps video gaming competitions will someday be part of the Olympics. You don't think so? Gaming is already considered a highly competitive sport with a strong following. You've heard of Major League Baseball? How about Major League Gaming (MLG; see http://www.mlgpro.com) complete with events, professionals, fans, sponsors, and media coverage? Then there is the Cyberathlete Professional League (CPL; http://www.thecpl.com/league/) which is the world's first video game sports league and has been the major force in the transformation of video game competitions to a professional sport. Over the past nine years, the CPL has hosted 50 international main events with a total attendance of 250,000 gamers, has sanctioned over 500 international qualifiers and has awarded $3,000,000 in prizes. As of ths writing, the Cyberathlete Amateur League (CAL), the CPL's online amateur division, has 500,000 registered members and hosts year-round online tournaments for over 60 game divisions.

Some gamers consider themselves professional athletes who follow highly rigorous and disciplined practice schedules. For instance, Johnathan Wendel, better known by the pseudonym Fatal1ty, is a professional electronic sports player who has won over US$1,000,000 in cash and prizes from professional competitions (You can see a video interview with Johnathan Wendel at http://www.youtube.com/watch?v=Q275Qh4ESao). In addition to receiving numerous product endorsements, he has been featured in mainstream news publications, including Time, The New York Times, Forbes, and the BBC World Service. He has also been featured on 60 Minutes. He is known as being one of the first professional gamers with a serious work ethic, and says he practices at least eight hours each day. Another professional gamer, Sam Suyeyasu, spends three to five hours a day blasting virtual enemies into oblivion with his Xbox. But at least one thing makes Suyeyasu very different: He's getting paid. Under the moniker of "Samurai," Suyeyasu and his gaming team, XiT Woundz, travel the country and compete for cash prizes. Throw in the $50 an hour fans pay him for private lessons, and he expects he'll clear $25,000 this year from gaming. Not too bad for a 19-year-old Californian who just earned his high-school equivalency diploma last year.[102]

In the not so distant future, I see professional gamers, cyberathletes if you will, dealing with some of the same issues as today's NBA basketball players, MLB baseball players, NHL hockey, and so on. Those with carpal tunnel syndrome will be put on the "injured list." Instead of steroids, they may be tested for Ritalin used to help them focus. We will take virtual tours of their "cribs" and watch online as their cars get "pimped." And some children will wonder why they need to work so hard in school when they can sit in front of a monitor and become wealthy and popular. Perhaps even a bit further in the future, cyberathletes will compete in large virtual, 3-dimensional, holographic rooms (arenas won't be needed because fans will cheer them on from virtual pubs in their homes). They will be required to show physical strength, agility, and athletic skills – a return to their roots among athletes in history. Because, as you know, the more things change, the more they stay the same.

Chapter 6: Human Solutions

Guarding kids from high-tech trouble is not a perfect science and comes with no 100% guarantee. In fact, I have consciously avoided the word "prevent" in this book so as not to give the wrong impression that, as parents and care takers, we can without failure completely shield our youth from the risks accompanying the use of high-tech tools. I prefer to use the more accurate and realistic term "risk reduction." Fully experiencing life comes with some risks. We send our children out into the world and help them achieve greater independence as they grow and mature. With each step of the way, they face greater challenges and dangers than the ones before them. We cannot be there for them every minute of every day. We cannot realistically sterilize the environment for them or restrict them to living in a "bubble." In fact, completely guarding kids from trouble actually robs them of important learning experiences which eventually shapes them into responsible and productive citizens. Many of our most enduring life lessons were learned only after successfully navigating trouble and resolving conflict.

One important aspect of our job as caretakers is allowing our children to experience situations with a bit of calculated risk from which they will learn valuable lessons – lessons that will serve them well into adulthood. We guide them through the lessons as effective teachers and mentors. As a result, our children are better able to make responsible decisions for themselves, especially in the face of risk. The reality of being a parent is that we cannot completely control other people, including our partners or even our children. Ultimately, they are responsible for their own behaviors. The best we can do is to develop respectful, trusting, and robust relationships with them so as to best influence them in a positive and effective way.

This chapter will help educators, parents, and caregivers understand the kinds of human or relational precautions they can take to better guard their kids from high-tech trouble. Chapter 7, *Technological Solutions*, focuses on additional solutions in the form of hardware and software that can also minimize the risk of exposing kids to inappropriate material and otherwise dangerous high-tech situations. No one solution will do. An appropriate combination of each – human/relational options as a primary method and high-tech solutions as backup – is ideal.

Human/Relational Precautions

You may not believe what I'm about to say, although here goes ... "You cannot control your children (nor can I control mine)." No matter what we say or do, ultimately, children will decide what they will do next. We have to teach them to make the best decisions they are capable of making, for themselves, while we are not around. In the meantime, we can focus on the things that we *do* control: the rules, structures, and consequences of our children's actions. Even then, they may choose to follow them or not depending on what they believe about the risks they take and the consequences that follow. This is not a book about parenting although when it comes to guarding kids in a high-tech world, I would like to offer a few brief tips.

Communication and Trust

Communication and trust are certainly very important processes in the context of overall effective parenting. When it comes to supervising children in a high-tech world, they are critical. Their exists a delicate balance between giving children their "space" or freedom to be autonomous and staying informed of what they are doing (i.e., supervising). To know *everything* that a child is up to is unrealistic and, I think, unnecessary. Yet, at the same time, as parents we fear that, at any given time, our children may be involved in an experience that puts them at risk without our knowledge. To complicate the matter, communication and trust are two relationship behaviors that are interdependent. That is, healthy communication leads to enhanced trust although, without trust, communication is difficult at best. When we engage in meaningful, caring, and positive communication, we experience this as "bonding." Our children believe that we understand them in their world. They perceive us as accepting and endearing. So how can adults facilitate a trusting relationship based on effective and appropriate communication? Tough question. The answer deserves much more space than allotted in this book although I do want to provide you with a few thoughts that should help.

First, let's take a look at what healthy communication is not. Especially with children, communication is not the same as interrogating, questioning, or lecturing which typically occur when the interaction stems from anger, suspicion, or guilt. Instead of being suspicious, be curious. Investigate the situation, not the child. Ask questions that help you learn, not help you to establish a case against the "accused" as if you were in a courtroom. If you find yourself using the word "you" a great deal, it probably sounds like an accusatory lecture which, more often than not, is a trust and communication killer. As much as possible, keep the focus on yourself by using the word "I" such as in, "I am worried about your level of safety when you chat online with others who I don't know." Also, "I wonder about how having a cell phone might distract you from homework?" Have relaxed conversations about your child's use of technology when the situation is calm, in the absence of any problems of issues. Do this from a point of being interested.

Understanding is also important. Kids need to understand that the rules and precautions you establish exist for their own safety and well-being. That it would probably be much easier on you to just let them do whatever they want although this would not be in their best interest or care. Explain to children this part of your job in a way they can comprehend and appreciate, using familiar analogies from everyday living. For instance, with middle and high school-aged students, you might use helpful analogies such as driving a car. No matter how skillful one is behind the wheel of a vehicle, one must still practice "defensive driving" and following the "rules of the road" to stay safe from the dangers posed by others who use the same roads. The overall message is, "I trust that you are responsible and cautious although I still worry about how others can hurt you."

GuardingKids.com

Negotiation

Some things are simply not negotiable such as letting a child cross a busy street by herself, without holding hands, at the age of, let's say, 5. Even though she may already be a good driver as evidenced by her high scores on the Crazy Taxi video game, you would probably just have to say "no" to letting your 9 year old take the family van out for a spin. What about getting a MySpace account? How about watching a PG-13 movie or chatting online? Should he really own his own cell phone? These questions are not as clear cut as the risk may not be as apparent. Yet, your child may have some logical and compelling arguments for doing these things that may be tough to debate. So when and how much do you give in? Here are some factors to consider and tips for deciding:

First, don't give in just because it's easier on you. Kids can wear you down although it's important to stay in the game and continue focusing on what is right. If you are tired, delay your decision until later, catch your breath, and think it over. Make sure your spouse or partner is "on board." If your child continues to engage, explain that asking more than twice is harassment and harassment is against the rules resulting in a default "no" and possible other consequences. If your child is not willing to wait for a decision, then again, the immediate answer is "no." If he is willing to wait for you to "take the decision under advisement," then negotiations may continue.

Second, realize that technology can be very powerful and extend our capabilities in incredible (and very much fun) ways. Let's remember, however, that *"Just because you can doesn't mean you should."* It is true that your child can stay in constant touch with his friends and get the latest gossip before it hits the streets. It is also true that she can correspond with almost anyone in the world. Although, *should* she? One of the ways to determine this is evaluating the purpose that the technology serves. What is your child trying to achieve by using the technology? For instance, what is the purpose of having a MySpace.com or other similar account? Ask questions such as, "What do you get out of being on MySpace?" If the answer is just that it's fun or that it helps the child stay more connected, then figure out how she can achieve that in a safer way. How about calling those would-be MySpace "friends" on the phone. What about a more private e-mail directly to the friend? Could the same goal be achieved by meeting at the park to hang out? Perhaps your child's rationale for having a social network account is to avoid being left out (i.e., "Everyone I know has one."). Although not having something that others have can be uncomfortable or unpleasant, it is not fatal. In fact, not having a social network account actually gives your child something that the other children do *not* have – more time and focus for other important things such as studies and family activities. You get the idea ... What purpose does a cell phone serve for a 6th grader or elementary school kid? Usually, cell phone ownership can be justified by the peace of mind extended to parents who can communicate with their children almost instantaneously. I agree, this is a wonderful advantage. But what about the potential pitfalls that I explained earlier in the book? This is the part of negotiation that begs for a compromise, a situation where everyone gets some of what they want although has to give up a little as well. This can lead to a win-win outcome. In the case of cell phone ownership, remember, the goal is to give the child the capability of anytime and anywhere communication with her parent/guardian and members of the emergency response community. This can be achieved by a limited use cellular phone, one that restricts the types of outgoing and incoming calls.

In the course of negotiations, remember to be objective. Be careful about allowing sensational stories propagated by the media to skew your judgement. Do your homework by investigating any technology by searching online and asking other parents. There are always *both* potential benefits and risks to using any technology. I've mentioned it earlier in the book, the value of technology is determined by its use, not the technology itself. A hammer can be used to build a house or commit a murder, depending on the users intentions. Assess the benefits versus the risks and whenever you deem it safe enough, do allow your child his request. Negotiating is never about control or the upper hand. Always keep in mind outcomes that are in the best interest of your child and how the negotiations can enhance your relationship. I would also add that allowing your child to deal with some reasonable risk can be a valuable learning experience and allows him to demonstrate to you that he is responsible. Realize too that rarely is anything in technology a "black or white" situation. Instead, technologies can usually be customized which allows your child to use them under certain conditions which you establish. For instance, perhaps you decide that your child may:

- Have an e-mail account that can only accept e-mails from people listed in the address book.

- Have an e-mail account although only you know the password and user identification.

- Have a MySpace account on the condition that it is set up as private and invitation only.

- Only use the Internet between certain hours of the day. Outside of those hours, your blocking/filtering software (eg., CyberSitter) shuts off the connection.

- May only use a web enabled gadget, including the computer, in plain view of an adult.

Third, as much as possible, focus more on what your child *can* do instead of what she cannot do. For instance, you may not allow your child to have their own cell phone although you may allow him to borrow yours now and then for special occasions. You may not allow your daughter to set up a MySpace account although you may allow her to set up her own blog which you monitor. Chatting using Yahoo! is a no-no although your kid may chat using http://xblock.isafe.org/chat.php.

Fourth, the same message may be easier to "swallow" if it came from someone else. If you can get another child, a friend, or other respected adult to relay the same message, it may carry more weight than coming from you.

Teaching Kids the "Rules of the Road"

Increasingly, schools have endeavored to provide children with knowledge, skills, and attitudes to effectively use technology to advance personal and educational goals. Although steady, their progress has been slow because technology competencies typically do not have the same priority as the traditional or "core" competencies of science, math, English, and social studies. The focus on high stakes testing has also made it difficult to make room in the curriculum or otherwise allot instruction time to appropriately give kids the training they need in the area of technology. Some parents believe that anything related to their child's education should be the responsibility of schools. Other parents have even relinquished some of their parental duties to their childrens' teachers and other educators. This is inappropriate, unrealistic, and, frankly, unfair. But, I digress a bit. For now, know that we as parents must not assume that others will help our children learn how to safely use high-tech tools. We need to do this in collaboration with educators (e.g., as part of a PTA meeting) or just do it ourselves.

Early on, our kids need to know that what applies in real life also applies in the virtual world of cyberspace. When approached by a stranger, they must ask for parent permission to speak to that person. This is important. Sexual predators and kidnappers are good at "grooming" children to trust them and eventually lure them into a dangerous situation. They take their time, determine the child's vulnerabilities, and then say just the right things that appeal to their sense of adventure. They reach out to their prey by instilling self-confidence and feelings of belongingness – the very same goals that we as parents strive to help our children achieve. In essence, they became parental figures with a sick motive. Or worse, they use their adult knowledge and resources to gain an unfair (and evil) advantage towards becoming the victim's "boyfriend" or "girlfriend." They follow the same process that rapists follow: First, enter the child's "personal space." They get to know the child and interact in friendly ways to create an illusion of trust. Second, they rely on the child ignoring any improprieties thus leading to a "slippery slope" of continued sexual banter and playfulness. Third, when the timing is right, they lure the child into isolation where there is little chance of others, especially adults, getting in the way. This can begin with a private one-on-one chat in the virtual world and may end up with a secluded meeting in the real world. Finally comes the assault.

Similar to the real world, talking to strangers online does not have to be forbidden, only supervised and monitored. To enforce a "forbid" policy is unrealistic and unnecessary. Not all strangers are evil, some do genuinely care. For instance, my own middle school child has developed a passion for photography. He became a member of an online (and family friendly) photography club who's members have encouraged and supported him in refining his photography skills. It would be impossible for me to conduct adequate background checks and meet every other member of the club. To deny him the interactions he has with the other members would also rob him of an excellent experience he has had, one that could easily influence a successful career for him as a professional photographer. Instead, I have interacted with the owners and topic moderators of the site who actually help me to monitor his online behavior. My son knows not to post any personal information which he is careful not to do. When he slips a bit, the website owners have done an excellent job of deleting any photos or other clues to his identity that he may unwittingly post. Except for a handful of frequent users on the site, I'm confident that the majority of members don't even know that he is a child. Of course, this is not enough. He registered on the site with an e-mail address that I monitor and so anytime he posts a message or receives one, I get an e-mail that lets me know exactly the nature of the posts (I'll share with you later in this section how I did this). I also have his account information and periodically enter to make sure he is still benefitting from the site in a safe and secure manner.

For your convenience, I have gleaned from various websites and from personal experience several other rules of the road that you should review and impress upon your child:

1. Never give out personal details such as your name, address or phone number. A corollary to this is never give out private details about your parents, family or friends. To a predator, these are clues to a puzzle that when finished, can help him/her determine who you are and even where you live. Also, family members may not want those details divulged for other reasons. For instance, a fun photo of "crazy" Uncle Joe at a party may get him in trouble with his boss or compromise his relationship with co-workers if it were discovered at work.

2. Never reveal passwords to your e-mail or other online accounts, even to your friends. Giving up your passwords means you give up control of the account which, for the purposes of our focus, is a security breach. Even trusted friends may accidentally do things online (e.g., send e-mails using your account) which may attract unwanted attention and open you up to the very kind of interactions you've been trying to avoid.

3. Never arrange to meet with anyone you have met online. If you think a meeting would benefit you, work with your parent to make it happen and only be present at the meeting with your parent.

4. Only put on your buddy list those "friends" approved by your parents. In fact, your online buddy list should be no longer than a list of your real life friends. And, parents should always meet and know the people on their child's buddy lists.

5. Never open any e-mail messages from others you don't recognize. It could very well contain a virus or inappropriate content. Even when you do recognize the name in the e-mail, don't open any attachments that you weren't expecting. Many viruses use a recipients address book to send out e-mails and even use first names as they appear in the address book to make the e-mail look genuine when it is really not.

6. Remember that people online may not be who they say they are, no matter how long you have been in contact with them. The Internet makes it very easy to conceal ones identity and masquerade as someone else. That 13 year old "friend" you have been interacting with could easily be a 45 year old man who intends to harm you.

7. If at any time you feel uncomfortable or uneasy, realize that something is probably wrong. Stop what you are doing (don't log off just yet) and get a parent or other trusted adult. The adult should save the message or evidence of the interaction and, if appropriate, use the content (including message headings) to report to the authorities. Also remember that it is not your fault if someone is trying to frighten you.

8. Do not reply to any bullying messages you receive. Bullies only take this as fuel for the fire and things could easily get worse. Instead, save and report to a trusted adult/parent.

9. Always abide by the "Golden Rule" when in chat rooms, talking on instant messenger, or sending e-mail—treat others the way you'd wish to be treated. Don't say anything to anyone that you wouldn't say on a stage or to a reporter.

10. Do not download or/and install any programs, especially file sharing software, without parental approval.

11. Be savvy when it comes to creating a user name. Ensure user names do not reveal too much personal information. It is inappropriate and dangerous for anyone to use his/her name or home town as their user name. Most user names made up of personal information are easily deciphered leading perpetrators to a child's identity and location.

12. No second chance for a first impression. Remember, people can copy and disseminate information to others so, even if information is deleted from a website, older versions may exist on others' computers. Think twice about what you post or send.

Online Instructional Modules

Help is available to you for teaching your children (and/or students) how to be as safe as possible in a high-tech world. In addition to having discussions, I recommend that you spend some time together on some websites designed for this very purpose. On these sites, you will find tutorials, quizzes, animated lessons, and more:

1. **NetSmartz**. The NetSmartz Workshop is an interactive, educational safety resource that teaches kids and teens how to stay safer on the Internet. NetSmartz combines the newest technologies available and the most current information to create high-impact educational activities that are well received by even the most tech-savvy kids. Parents, guardians, educators, and law enforcement also have access to additional resources for learning and teaching about the dangers children may face online. NetSmartz was created by the National Center for Missing & Exploited Children® (NCMEC) and Boys & Girls Clubs of America (BGCA). http://www.netsmartz.org/

2. **Don't Believe the Type**. This information was adapted from Teen Safety on the Information Highway written by Lawrence J. Magid, a syndicated columnist, media commentator, and host of www.safekids.com and www.safeteens.com. He is also the author of The Little PC Book (Peach Pit Press, 1993). http://tcs.cybertipline.com/

3. **GetNetWise**. The Internet is an increasingly important place to work, play and learn for both adults and children. At the same time, we are concerned about the risks we face online. The challenge is to stay "one-click" ahead of would-be pornographers, hackers, child-predators and those who would misuse your and your child's sensitive information. GetNetWise can help. http://www.getnetwise.org/

4. **Internet Safety for Teachers**. Although designed for teachers, you as a parent can use this site which is designed to educate children about the dangers that lurk online. Here you will find free interactive lessons you can use at home as well as in your classroom. http://www.safekids.ne.gov/teachers.html

5. **Internet Superheroes**. Delivering smart, safe and responsible surfing messages to children, teens, schools and parents, online and offline. http://www.internetsuperheroes.com/

6. **Kidsmart**. Kidsmart is an award winning practical Internet safety program website for schools, young people, parents, and agencies, produced by the children's Internet charity Childnet International. http://www.kidsmart.org.uk/

7. **Chatdanger**. A site all about the potential dangers on interactive services online like chat, IM, online games, e-mail and on mobiles. Click on the icons below to read TRUE STORIES and find out how to chat SAFELY... http://www.chatdanger.com/

8. **GuardingKids.com**. More educational resource links at the website.

Supervision

"Hold hands while crossing the street" is good advice in reality and makes perfect sense in the virtual world as well. Adult supervision is a primary method for guarding our children from high-tech risk, more effective than the most advanced technology yet developed for this purpose. There exists no substitute for sitting down with your kids and exploring the World Wide Web together. This is true when surfing for leisure, doing homework, or conducting education related activities. Similar to watching television together, adults and children who surf the Web together share an experience which can prove to be beneficial to the relationship. Further, the Web provides much opportunity for discussing scores of topics and issues favorable for learning. Besides, if you are an educator and a student or class in your custody accesses pornographic material on the Net because you were not appropriately supervising, you may place yourself and your school at legal risk and consequently endanger your career. More specifically, consider the following suggestions:

Keep the Computer in a Visible Area. Isolation is the key to getting in trouble. Perpetrators know on some level that if they are to succeed in their victimization, they need to first pick a vulnerable victim (sometimes, kids are vulnerable just because they are kids) and remove any potential intervening factors. Intervening factors can include both other adults in close proximity and knowing the perpetrator's identity. You need to be that intervening factor by always being a few feet away. You can do this by keeping the Internet connected computer monitor in a public area of your house, perhaps the living room or off the kitchen. If you don't have an Internet connection near that public location in your house, you may have to install a router and "drop" one in. This is the most secure and best way to preserve your connection speed. A more practical way to go is to install a secure wireless router. If you are not sure how to set up a wireless connection, consult with your local electronics store salesperson who can probably help (or check out http://www.microsoft.com/athome/moredone/wirelesssetup.mspx).

Help Supervise at School. I remember doing an online chat with parents not too long ago at a local television station while they did a story about guarding kids online. What struck me about the chat was how many parents wanted to complain about how their childrens' schools were not doing enough to protect them while using Internet connected computers (usually after explaining that their son or daughter witnessed inappropriate material while online at school). I told them what I wrote here earlier – that this kind of work does not come with a 100% guarantee. In fact, when challenged, my local school district explained that there are millions of new adult oriented and otherwise inappropriate sites that currently exist. Even if our filtering technologies are 99% effective, that means thousands of sites can still end up in plain view, right in front of our youngsters. Also, remember that the Internet is a dynamic place where sites and content is changing every second of every day. It's literally a moving target which no filtering/blocking software can perfectly deal with. What is also needed is human intervention. We need to take turns and volunteer to help monitor what our students are doing when they are using Internet connected computers at school. No one teacher, not even with a couple of assistants, can effectively do this in a classroom of 25-40 students. Work with your child's teacher to help children benefit from the wonderful educational tools that others offer on the Internet while staying safe and secure.

Get Techno-Literate Yourself

"Every time I get with the program, someone changes the channel." I've heard several variations of this over the years from many of the adults I have worked with. Chances are that you are overwhelmed at the thought of learning about technology, I do understand. In fact, because a significant part of my career has focused on counseling technology, I often feel like I have to keep up with two areas of discipline: professional counseling and educational technology. However, there is some good news. First of all, you don't have to learn it all at once. Develop a series of goals for yourself that includes small and consistent steps towards an overall program of "keeping up." You have already started by reading this book. Take what you've learned here, use the supplementary websites and references, and continue advancing your knowledge and skills a little bit each day. Before you know it, you'll be speaking "bytes" and "gigs" with the rest of us. Here are some other tips for developing your techno-literacy:

- Subscribe to e-mail newsletters (most are free) that focus on helping you become more technologically literate. This way, the tips and tricks for dealing with technology come to you in a manageable way. For instance, some of the more popular periodic newsletters include:
  - Technology Horizons in Education (T.H.E.) is a free magazine for educators dedicated to technology solutions in education. http://www.thejournal.com/
  - Edutopia Magazine gives practical, hands-on insight into what works, what's on the horizon, and who is shaping the changing future of education. http://www.edutopia.org/

- ResearchBuzz is designed to cover the world of Internet research. To that end this site provides almost daily updates on search engines, new data managing software, browser technology, large compendiums of information, Web directories — whatever. If in doubt, the final question is, "Would a reference librarian find it useful?" If the answer's yes, in it goes!. http://www.researchbuzz.com/

- Ask Bob Rankin about computers, viruses, spyware, search engines or almost anything about the Internet. http://www.askbobrankin.com/

- Technology tips and news from Kim Komando, the "Digital Goddess." http://www.komando.com/

- On-Line Technology Tutorials From Around the World Wide Web. http://www.internet4classrooms.com/on-line2.htm

- Internet for Information and Communication Technology (A free, "teach yourself" tutorial that lets you practice your Internet Information Skills). http://www.vts.rdn.ac.uk/tutorial/ict

- Interview your child about the latest and greatest technologies from his/her perspective. Ask as if you don't know such as, "I heard someone on the radio the other day talking about how he was listening to his podcast, do you know what that is?" You may be surprised to learn just how much your child understands (after they get over the shock of you using the techno-lingo).

- Use any popular search engine with keywords presented in this book (e.g., social network, cell phone and children, iPod, etc.) and add the word "tutorial" which will result in all kinds of valuable demonstrations and instructions. I have also found that the keywords "parenting technology" [without the quotes] work very well at uncovering valuable resources.

- Go online as if you were a child. Search blog sites children frequent to see what information they are posting and use search engines or other sources to find out what it all means.

- Take a class at a local community college or vocational/technical school. Perhaps you might even enroll *with* your child and make it a shared experience.

- Learn how to use your computer in your own home, at your own pace, on your own schedule by using computer training software. For instance, I enjoy products from http://www.599cd.com.

- Check out Online Technology Tutorials from the Kent School District, Washington. http://www.kent.k12.wa.us/KSD/IT/TSC/prof_dev/tutorials.html

Technology is changing every day and so it's important to keep up and stay aware as much as possible. This isn't easy although nobody said that effective parenting was easy.

Check Your Child's Web Presence

Every now and then (I do it every couple of months or so), you may want to conduct online searches that may lead to information about your child posted by him/her or someone else. For example, use a meta-search engine such as jux2 (http://www.jux2.com/) which can compare Google, Yahoo, and MSN search results to see what type of web presence your child has (and if it is safe or not). Use keywords such as a userid or e-mail address that your child is using. Use his name both within quotes and without quotes around them (the difference being how the search engine treats the search, either as two keywords or a phrase). Use his/her name in combination with other personal information such as school name or hometown name to narrow the search down a bit if it is too general.

If your child has information posted somewhere such as a website, use Google's backward links feature to see if others are linked to that information. Simply put in "link:" right before the website address. For example, if you were to do a backwards link check of my site, you would enter link:www.guardingkids.com as the search term.

Finally, you may want to check some specialized search engines that index parts of the Web that other search engines may miss:

- **Technorati** is the recognized authority on what's happening on the World Live Web, right now. The Live Web is the dynamic and always-updating portion of the Web. We search, surface, and organize blogs and the other forms of independent, user-generated content (photos, videos, voting, etc.) increasingly referred to as "citizen media." as of this writing, Technorati is tracking 112.8 million blogs and over 250 million pieces of tagged social media. http://technorati.com/about/

- **Google Group** is a place where users create and own their own online community. http://groups.google.com/. Also check out Yahoo! Groups at http://groups.yahoo.com

GuardingKids.com

- **Google Blog Search** is a Google search technology focused on blogs. http://blogsearch.google.com/

- **del.icio.us** is a social bookmarking website – the primary use of del.icio.us is to store your bookmarks online, which allows you to access the same bookmarks from any computer and add bookmarks from anywhere, too. On del.icio.us, you can use tags to organize and remember your bookmarks, which is a much more flexible system than folders. http://del.icio.us

Teach Your Child to Prioritize

Being productive in today's fast paced world requires excellent time and resource management. It also requires a great deal of focus because there are so many intriguing distractions that can potentially derail our efforts to accomplish our goals. Allocating time to different tasks, working on self-imposed deadlines, and prioritizing among goals are key skills for being successful. In addition, setting boundaries around "what" and "how" we choose to accomplish is key, especially in light of the fact that technology tends to blur or diminish boundaries and introduce chaos. How do children learn these skills? Well, like everything else, they learn them through formal education (school) and informally, through watching others exercise these skills. You as parent or guardian must make certain that your child develops these important set of skills. Here are a few websites that can help:

- **What is the point of time management tips?** Changing time management habits takes time and effort, and it is always much easier when you have a simple system of practical rules and hints that are easy to keep in mind. That is exactly what the tips on this page are about. http://www.time-management-guide.com/time-management-tips.html

- **Stop Stressing Six Ways To Prioritize Your Work.** http://tinyurl.com/39kcpe

- **Time Management: Setting Goals and Priorities** from the University of Florida Counseling Center. http://tinyurl.com/3ak7xb

- **A To Do List That Works** by F. John Reh. http://management.about.com/cs/yourself/a/ToDoList1002.htm

- **Time Management** from PBS. If you learn to tame the time monster, you might be surprised at how much you can get done. The real reward, however, is that you'll probably feel less stressed and more happy. http://pbskids.org/itsmylife/school/time/

- **Time Management from Mind Tools.** Beat work overload. Increase your effectiveness. Achieve much more. http://www.mindtools.com/pages/main/newMN_HTE.htm
- **Managing Your Time from Dartmouth College.** This website also includes free downloadable resources. http://www.dartmouth.edu/~acskills/success/time.html

Understand the Code: The New Shorthand

You walk over to your child while she is on a computer chatroom, IM, or as they are "chatting" on their cell phone and you notice that she writes, "POS CUL8R." You assume such gibberish is a mistake or shrug it off as silly pre-adolescent banter. It probably is, no different than how you and I operated at that age. Although if you knew that these acronyms stood for "Parent Over Shoulder See You Later," you may want to know more about what she is talking about to better determine her level of safety. Some "codes" may be more alerting than others. What if you noticed your child receiving shorthand such as ASL or TDTM. The first asks for "Age, Sex, and Location" and the second stands for "Talk Dirty to Me" – two very commonly used abbreviations from others who may very well have disingenuous motives.

Children (and some adults) have developed their own type of shorthand to quickly keep up with the pace of communication in chatrooms, on cell phones, and via instant messaging. When the "room" is filled with 20, 30, or more people, the conversation can be fast and furious. In the case of cell phone text messaging, the "keyboard" or dial pad is very small and cumbersone which also leads to the need to be brief and concise. Some chat or other messaging environments do not support multimedia exchanges which limit users in how they can express themselves beyond simple words. These limitations of time and technology have spawned a new set of acronyms and symbols. What some children have also discovered is that the same language may be effective in communicating with other children while keeping their parents "in the dark." The bad news for parents is that these symbols may be difficult to decipher without continued exposure and practice. While participating in some fast paced chatrooms, I still have to keep a computer lingo dictionary or online converter open just to keep up. Its like being in a foreign country and you don't speak the language. Here are a few websites that should help:

- http://www.city-net.com/~ched/help/lingo/jargonlinks.html
- http://www.web-friend.com/help/lingo/chatslang.html
- http://www.stands4.com/
- http://da.co.la.ca.us/pok/poklist.htm

Also, check out http://www.netlingo.com/ for some helpful lists such as *The NetLingo Top 20 Internet Acronyms Every Parent Needs to Know* and *50 More Internet Acronyms Every Parent Should Know.*

Emoticons and Smileys

Emoticons are symbols (icons) used to express emotion, thus the hybrid word emoticon, a cross between emotions an icons. The idea is to turn your head sideways, usually to the left, and you'll notice a sort of rudimentary picture of a face with a certain smile, each one depicting a certain mood. For instance, ;-) is one where the ; (semi-colon) are the eyes, the - is the nose, and the) is the mouth. Also, you see some people use the hyphen (-) to show the nose, while others will show the same expression without the nose. Example: ;-) and ;) signify the same thing. Other times, keyboard characters can form basic pictures such as [_]> which depicts a cup of coffee (keep your head straight on this one). Some chat rooms will convert text based emoticons such as the ones I just mentioned into actual graphics. Other emoticons, also known as smileys or winks, are animated. And yet others, are innappropriate because they depict characters of a sexual nature. Unfortunately, some emoticons are quite explicit such as depicting various sexual positions and more, for example (see http://www.myemoticons.com/adultemoticons/adult.htm or http://www.msnemotions.org/emoticon.25.Naughty-Emoticons.html). Remember, a picture (or symbol) may be worth a thousand words, none of which you may want your child to hear.

LeetSpeak

Leetspeak, or leet for short, is a specific type of computer slang in which a user replaces regular letters with other keyboard characters to form words phonetically. Though it was originally used by computer hackers and online gamers ("leet" is a vernacular form of "elite"), leet has moved into the Internet mainstream. Your kids might use it online for fun, and you might even have seen a word or two used by your own friends and associates online. Leet words can be expressed in hundreds of ways, using different substitutions and combinations. Nearly all characters are formed as phonemes and symbols, so with a bit of practice leet can be fairly easy to translate. However, leet is not a formal or regional dialect; any given word can be interpreted differently by different groups of people. [103]

For example the word "leet" in leetspeak would become "1337".

Would you know what this online chat was about?

Mary: |-|0\/\/ r j00Z?
Jill: pH1I\I3, \/\/|-|47'5 UP \/\/17|-| j00Z?
Mary: I\I07 /\/\U(|-|.
Jill: 937 j00R |-|0/\/\3\/\/0RI< pH1I\I15|-|3D '/37?
Mary: '/35.
Jill: j00Z 901I\I9 70 $73\/3'5 p4R'/ 7|-|15 \/\/33I<3I\ID?
Mary: I\I07 5UR3 '/37, |-|4\/3 70 45I< /\/\'/ / \/\/0/\/\. $I-|3'LL pR0B4BL'/ 54'/ I\I0. $U(I<5.
Jill: '/34, /\/\3 700.
Mary: |-|34RD pHR0/\/\ 70/\/\ '/37?
Jill: '/35, |-|4D 4 L4/\/\3 (0I\I\/3R54710I\I, 73LL j00Z 4B0U7 17 L473R.
Mary: 4LR19|-|7, |-|4\/3 70 90.
Jill: $33 j00Z L473R.
Mary: B'/3.

Use the Following Translator to help you decipher the message:

a = 4 or @ or /-\
b = 8 or |3
c = (or ¢ or k
d = <| or [)
e = 3 or &
f = |= or ph
g = 6 or 9 or &
h = # or [-] or {=}
j = ,| or _| or ;
i = 1 or & or 3y3
k = |< or /<
l = | or 1
m = |\/| or ^^ or |v|
n = |\| or <\>
o = 0 or ¤
p = |^ or |* or |o or 9
q = 9 or (,)
r = |2 or P\
s = 5 or $ or z
t = 7 or +
u = you
u = |_| or (_) or |_| or v
v = \/ or \/ or <
w = // or \/\/ or \^/ or (n) or \V/
x = ><
y = '/ or `/ or V/ or ¥ or % '/
z= 2 or S
l8r = later
n00b = newbie
r0x0r = rocks
skillz = skills
u2 = you too
w00t = woohoo

If you need to cheat, you can at anytime by copying some leetspeak into an online converter such as the one found at http://www.brenz.net/l337Maker.asp

The answer:

Mary: How are you?
Jill: Fine, what's up with you?
Mary: Not much.
Jill: Get your homework Finished yet?
Mary: Yes.
Jill: You going to steve's pary this weekend?
Mary: Not sure yet, have to ask my mom. She'll probably say no. Sucks.
Jill: Yea, me too.
Mary: Heard from Tom yet?
Jill: Yes, had a lame conversation, tell you about it later.
Mary: Alright, have to go.
Jill: See you later.
Mary: Bye.

Legislation to Help Protect Children

At this point, you may be wondering how it could be that so many crimes in real life can so easily be committed in cyberspace? Selling drugs, pedaling child porn, sexual predatory behavior, etc. seems to run rampant in the online world, how come? The nature of Internet pornography, indecency, obscenity, and the sort of person who uses it has resulted in a war that is being waged on the Internet, in children's homes, and certainly on Capitol Hill. The debate has raised not only questions of what exactly is obscenity, harassment, free speech, and censorship, but also of government control over the Internet. In other words, technology has forced us to question what we have always assumed about some very important ideas and made us face the precious balance between democracy and safety. Also, federal and state laws that appropriately delineates actions and consequences has not kept up with the pace of developing technology. We see this in all aspects of our lives. There is more technology available than we know what to do with and how to manage. Yet another reason for legislative inadequacy deals with the enforcement aspect. Because technology is everywhere, sexual predators and other criminals are more of a "moving target" than ever before. They can support their criminal behavior from just about anywhere and at any time of the day or night. The authorities simply do not have the necessary human and financial resources to stay one step ahead.

Whatever legislation ends up being imposed in this arena, it will set a precedent for how the government deals with the exchange of information in the future. Is the Internet a free forum for discussion, or is it a broadcasting service, and therefore subject to the same restrictions as television, print, or radio? Are communications on the Internet covered by the right to privacy? And who is accountable for what happens on it?

Although more slowly than we would like, legislation continues to further the cause of protecting children online. Following is a summary of several major laws of which to be aware (in chronological order of enactment) and accompanying websites for further details. Then, I would like to increase your awareness of other efforts and remind you to take action by participating in the legislative process.

The Communications Decency Act (CDA)

The Communications Decency Act (CDA) attempted to regulate obscenity in cyberspace and how indecency might be available to children. A second section of the Act declared that operators of Internet services were not to be construed as publishers (and thus legally liable for the words of third parties who use their services). Many people found the CDA unconstitutional, and its passing prompted an Internet-wide protest. As a result, the CDA was challenged and overturned, and then taken to the Supreme court where on June 26, 1997 it was soundly defeated on the basis of it being unconstitutional.

http://www.fcc.gov/Speeches/Chong/separate_statements/cda.txt

http://en.wikipedia.org/wiki/Communications_Decency_Act

Child Online Protection Act (COPA)

The Child Online Protection Act (COPA) is a law in the United States of America, passed in 1998, which declared the purpose of protecting children from harmful sexual material on the Internet. The law was blocked by the courts and has never taken effect. Because it only limited commercial speech and only affected U.S. providers, the effect on the availability of the regulated material to minors if the law was enforced was unlikely to be significant. Several U.S. states have since passed similar laws.

http://en.wikipedia.org/wiki/Child_Online_Protection_Act

http://www.epic.org/free_speech/censorship/copa.html

Children's Online Privacy Protection Act of 1998 (COPPA)

The Children's Online Privacy Protection Act, effective April 21, 2000, applies to the online collection of personal information from children under 13. The rules spell out what a Website operator must include in a privacy policy, when and how to seek verifiable consent from a parent and what responsibilities an operator has to protect children's privacy and safety online.

http://www.coppa.org/

http://www.copacommission.org/report/

The Children's Internet Protection Act (CIPA)

The Children's Internet Protection Act (CIPA), signed into law on December 21, 2000, requires that schools and libraries that receive specified federal funding certify that they have in place an Internet safety policy that includes monitoring the use of Internet access by children and implementation of technology that will filter out objectionable content. On May 31, 2002, in the U.S. District Court for the Eastern Division of Pennsylvania, CIPA was declared facially unconstitutional (i.e.., in the Court's opinion, the law cannot be applied in a constitutional manner). The District Court decision changed the requirements of CIPA by suspending the technology protection measure for public libraries although not for schools. Then on June 23, 2003, the U.S. Supreme Court declared that CIPA *is* facially constitutional and can be applied in a constitutional manner – a reversal of the previous decision in Pennsylvania.

http://www.fcc.gov/cgb/consumerfacts/cipa.html

http://www.fcc.gov/Bureaus/Common_Carrier/Orders/2001/fcc01120.doc

Deleting Online Predators Act of 2006 (DOPA)

Introduced on May 9th, 2006, the Deleting Online Predators Act sought to amend the Communications Act of 1934 to require recipients of universal service support for schools and libraries to protect minors from commercial social networking websites and chat rooms. According to the proposed legislation, the bill prohibits access by minors without parental authorization to a commercial social networking website or chat room through which minors may easily access or be presented with obscene or indecent material; may easily be subject to unlawful sexual advances, unlawful requests for sexual favors, or repeated offensive comments of a sexual nature from adults may easily access other material that is harmful to minors.

This bill too was heavily debated as it faced several criticisms: First, it uses broad definitions of "online social network" which may impede legitimate and appropraate commercial blogging tools and e-mail list services. Second, the Bill does have provisions for allowing educational uses of online social networks. The legislation states that the filtering may be switched off "during use by an adult or by minors with adult supervision to enable access for educational purposes." However, some wonder whether schools will allow educators to deactivate the filter to allow such access, that is, letting educators make decisions over which sites get filtered and when. In July 2006, this bill passed the House of Representatives although died in the Senate. In January of 2007, the DOPA bill resurfaced in the form of another piece of proposed legislation entitled Protecting Children in the 21st Century Act or sometimes referred to as DOPA, Jr. As of this writing, this bill has been read twice and referred to the Committee on Commerce, Science, and Transportation.

http://www.techlawjournal.com/cong109/bills/house/hr5319/hr5319ih.asp

http://thomas.loc.gov/cgi-bin/query/z?c109:H.R.5319:

http://en.wikipedia.org/wiki/Deleting_Online_Predators_Act

Other Important Initiatives

Internet Corporation For Assigned Names and Numbers (ICANN)

Although not state or federal government, the Internet Corporation For Assigned Names and Numbers (ICANN) is an internationally organized, non-profit corporation that has responsibility for Internet Protocol (IP) address space allocation, protocol identifier assignment, generic (gTLD) and country code (ccTLD) Top-Level Domain name system management, and root server system management functions. This is a lot of technobabble to describe the group that governs how the Internet works, including what you type into your browser to get to a specific site or domain. Remember, the Domain Name System (DNS) helps users find their way around the Internet. Every computer on the Internet has a unique address called its "IP address" (Internet Protocol address). Because IP addresses (which are strings of numbers) are hard to remember, the DNS allows a familiar string of letters (the "domain name") to be used instead. So rather than typing "192.0.34.163," you can type "www.icann.org."

In recent years, ICANN has been struggling with the decision to establish a XXX domain for pornography (which means all adult oriented websites addresses would end in .xxx), essentially creating a "red light district" on the Internet. One advantage of this domain is that it would be much easier to block sites by just preventing any site within this domain from showing up, not as much dependence on analyzing site content. In November 2000, the ICANN staff objected to the .xxx domain and explained that determining which sites are included or excluded, given the international reach and complexity of the Internet, would be too troublesome. (Similar arguments were made for establishing a .kids domain which would include only those sites deemed safe and appropriate for children.) Politicians quickly lambasted the 2000 decision. At a hearing a few months later, Rep. Fred Upton, R-Mich., demanded to know why ICANN didn't approve .xxx "as a means of protecting our kids from the awful, awful filth, which is sometimes widespread on the Internet." Sen. Joseph Lieberman, D-Conn., complained to a federal commission that .xxx was necessary to force adult Webmasters to "abide by the same standard as the proprietor of an X-rated movie theater."

In June of 2006, ICANN approved .xxx domains, a move that reversed the group's earlier position. Now the organization is receiving a great deal of pressure to head off the decision once again. For instance, Michael Gallagher, assistant secretary at the Commerce Department, has asked for a hold to be placed on the contract to run the new top-level domain until the .xxx suffix can receive further scrutiny. A letter sent from ICANN's government advisory group asks for a halt to "allow time for additional governmental and public policy concerns to be expressed before reaching a final decision." The Family Research Council, for instance, warned that "pornographers will be given even more opportunities to flood our homes, libraries and society with pornography through the .xxx domain." How this new domain pans out still remains to be seen.

http://www.icann.org/

http://en.wikipedia.org/wiki/ICANN

GuardingKids.com

Internet Crimes Against Children (ICAC) Program

Operational since 1998, the ICAC Task Force Program was created to help State and local law enforcement agencies enhance their investigative response to offenders who use the Internet, online communication systems, or other computer technology to sexually exploit children. The program is currently composed of 46 regional Task Force agencies and is funded by the United States Office Of Juvenile Justice and Delinquency Prevention. The Training & Technical Assistance Program was established to assist these agencies with training and technical assistance in support of their Internet Crimes Against Children initiatives.

http://www.icactraining.org/

Project Safe Childhood (PSC)

On February 15th, 2006, Alberto R. Gonzales (former Attorney General) announced Project Safe Childhood (PSC), a Department of Justice initiative aimed at preventing the abuse and exploitation of kids through the Internet. PSC will be modeled on the blueprint of the successful Project Safe Neighborhoods (PSN) initiative, a nationwide program started in 2001 to reduce gun crime in America. PSN provided a comprehensive enforcement strategy for deterring and punishing gun crimes by linking together federal, state, local, and tribal law enforcement, prosecutors, community leaders, and non-profit entities specializing in prevention and outreach. By establishing a network of law enforcement and community initiatives directed at gun violence, PSN enhanced the coordination among law enforcement at all levels. U.S. Attorneys in the 94 federal judicial districts worked with the Bureau of Alcohol, Tobacco, Firearms and Explosives, and with state, local, and tribal law enforcement officials, to tailor the PSN strategy to the unique needs of the local gun violence problem. Each district has coordinated prosecutions under federal, state, and local laws; ensured that law enforcement officers and prosecutors receive the proper training; and engaged in deterrence and prevention efforts through community outreach and awareness campaigns. [104]

http://www.projectsafechildhood.gov/

http://www.usdoj.gov/opa/pr/2006/February/06_opa_081.html

School Acceptable Use Policies (AUP)

With Internet access now a staple of most schools, it is critical that a clear set of guidelines for the use of the resources that this access provides are needed for the guidance of the students, teachers, administrators, parents, and board members. Using the Internet such as with supplementing classroom instruction can be somewhat risky. It is advisable to obtain consent forms from all parents at the beginning of the school year emphasizing that, while all efforts will be directed toward seeing that children access appropriate material, common sense dictates that no monitoring system is foolproof, and in the final analysis students must also assume responsibility for accessing only appropriate material. An Acceptable Use Policy is a document which establishes parameters for those who use the Internet at school. The document addresses appropriate use of the school's system, the rights of all parties involved, protocols and procedures for infractions, and liabilities such as in the case of loss or damage. The AUP includes definitions of acceptable online behavior and access privileges. Parents and educators should definitely pay attention to their childrens' school AUP. [105]

How to Advocate

There are many wonderful websites available that can help you to add your voice to the many others so that, in great numbers, we can instill global change to help guard our kids against high-tech trouble. These websites will help you do everything from inform others about Internet safety to advocating for for new legislation:

Becoming an Advocate (from the National Peace Corp Association). This website discusses the various things that one can do to become a successful advocate. Particularly helpful is how they provide information for how to work with a Member of Congress. http://www.rpcv.org/pages/sitepage.cfm?id=732

National Center for Missing & Exploited Children. This website is a must-see. Here, you will find volunteer and outreach opportunities while also staying informed of up-to-date information regarding the safety and security of children. http://www.missingkids.com/

Congress.org is a service of Capitol Advantage and Knowlegis, LLC; private, non-partisan companies that specialize in facilitating civic participation. This website will help you stay up on political issues, contact your congressmen, and voice your opinons. http://www.congress.org/

United States Senate. The official page of the United States Senate. http://www.senate.gov/

United States Congress. The official page of the United States Congress. http://www.house.gov/

GuardingKids.com

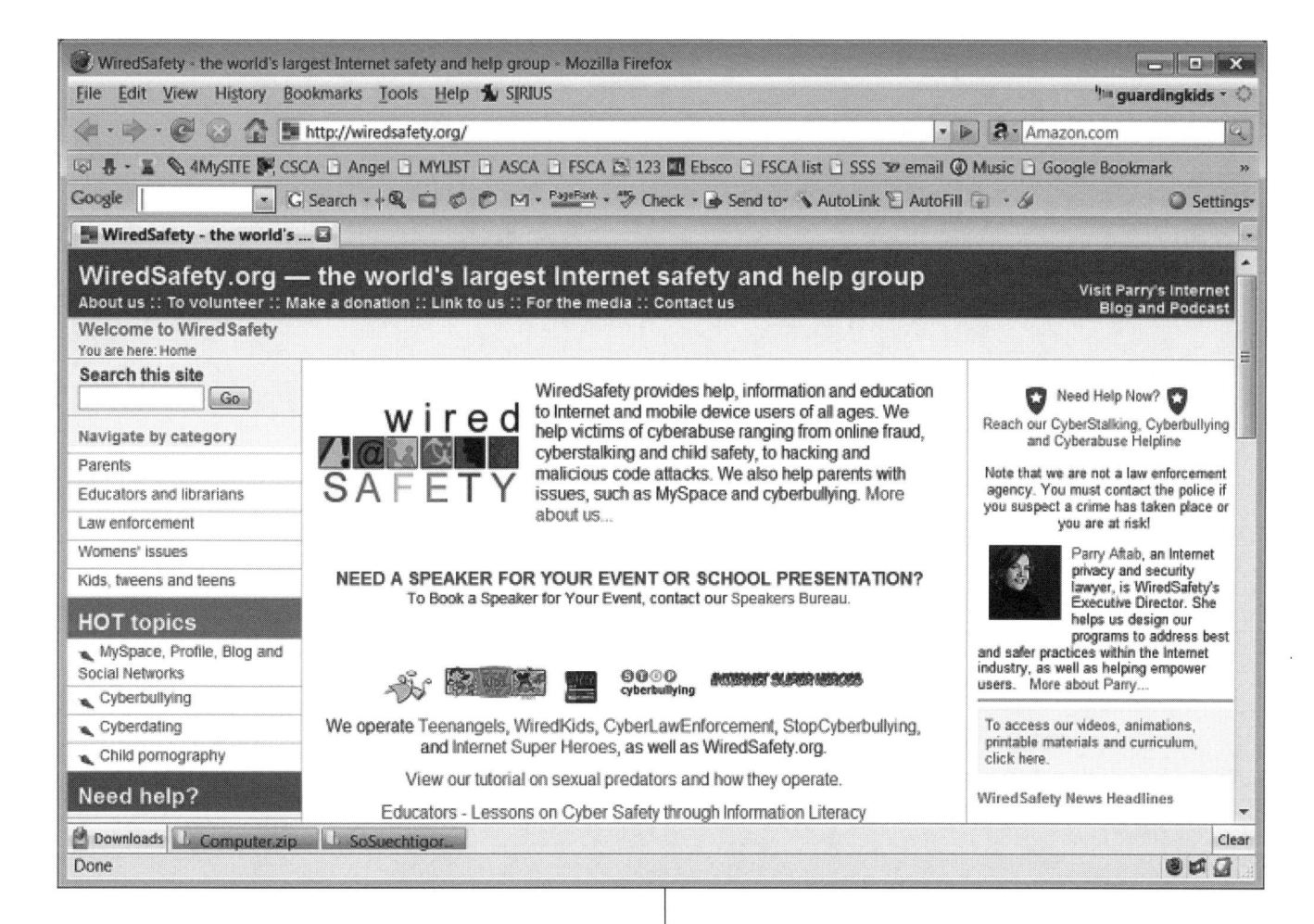

WiredSafety.org has volunteer opportunities. WiredSafety, is the largest online safety, education and help group in the world. They are a "cyber-neighborhood watch" and operate worldwide in cyberspace through their more than 9,000 volunteers worldwide. http://www.wiredsafety.org/volunteer/

Library of Congress (LOC). The purpose of thes website it to make federal legislative information freely available to the public. http://thomas.loc.gov/

Bully Police USA. A Watch-dog Organization - Advocating for Bullied Children & Reporting on State Anti Bullying Laws. http://www.bullypolice.org/

Chapter 7: Technological Solutions

Monitoring and approving all high-tech interactions is, realistically, very difficult at best if not humanly impossible. Therefore, adequately guarding kids from harmful material requires both human *and* technological assistance. A combination of hardware, software, and human effort provides very reasonable security which should help us sleep better at night knowing that appropriate boundaries have been restored. Following are several technologically based measures from which you can choose. Each focuses on a different risk although can be effective in guarding kids in one or more areas. For instance, anti-pop-up software can help prevent exposure to pornography, inappropriate websites, and potential viruses. Today's filtering/blocking software will be a primary precaution for many of the risks overviewed in this book.

Before continuing, however, I do want to re-emphasize that technological solutions to guarding kids is not a replacement for human intervention. We need to help children be knowledgeable about the use (and misuse) of technology, teach them how to make good decisions about how they use technology, and help them police themselves (and perhaps each other) when they are "off track." Technological solutions are, in my opinion, an effective secondary measure or backup to how we prepare and supervise our children otherwise. In no particular order, here are some viable solutions you can implement right away:

Pop-Ups

Remember, pop-ups are those pesky little windows that "pop up" while you are browsing. Some will open as soon as the web page you are visiting finishes downloading, others will come up when hovering your mouse cursor over a link, and yet others will open upon leaving the page. They often contain advertising information or worse, bombard you with one pornographic website after another. They are difficult to deal with because the windows open without any buttons to close. Even if you can close a pop-up, frequently another one or more opens right up in its place. The good news is that Pop-Ups have significantly declined as a problem or issue for several reasons. First, they are so annoying that companies that used them were experiencing the opposite effect – users would shy away from the website or worse, boycot the company or website altogether. Second, software became increasingly more powerful for blocking pop-ups which meant that these companies were wasting their time withe content that was rarely viewed. That is, the effectiveness of pop-ups has been greatly compromised. However, they still exist which means that its still a good idea to incorporate anti-pop-up solutions.

Usually the only way to stop pop-ups is to close the browser by clicking on the red "X" in the top right corner or, in Windows, hold the Alt key and press F4 very quickly to close these windows at a rapid pace. Another more effective way to prevent pop-ups altogether is to install a program (usually free) called a pop-up blocker. Here are several:

- Most search engine toolbars such as the Google Toolbar (http://toolbar.google.com/) or Yahoo! Toolbar (http://toolbar.yahoo.com/) includes a pop-up blocker for the Internet Explorer browser;

- If you're using Windows XP and have the Service Pack 2 (SP2) installed (http://www.microsoft.com/windowsxp/sp2/default.mspx), you have a pop-up blocker. When you install SP2, Pop-up Blocker is turned on in Internet Explorer and set to the medium setting, which means it will block most automatic pop-ups. The default settings for the pop-up blocker allow you to see pop-ups that are opened when you click a link or button on a website. Pop-up Blocker will also play a sound and show the Information Bar when a pop-up is blocked. You can adjust these settings so that Pop-up Blocker works the way you want it to.

- Another popular pop-up stopper that works with both Internet Explorer is called Pop-Up Stopper® Free Edition (http://www.panicware.com/product_psfree.html). The Professional version works with other such as the increasingly popular Firefox, AOL, MSN, Mozilla Firefox, Netscape 4.x, 6.x, 7.x, Opera 6.x - 7.x, SBC Yahoo, WMConnect, CompuServe, Juno, NetZero, Mozilla 1.7.3 or older.

- Other free pop-up blockers can be found at http://www.popuptest.com/software/freeware_popblock.html

It doesn't hurt to have a couple of these running at the same time. I have found that the pop-up blockers that come with the Google Toolbar and Internet Explorer 7.0 running at the same time have solved the problem for me almost entirely. Once you've installed your blockers, you can test them out by visiting http://www.popuptest.com/.

Blocking and Filtering Software

Software solutions to preventing access to harmful material falls into two general classes. Solutions that (a) block net access to certain addresses deemed to contain objectionable material (i.e., blocking); and (b) block access based on the appearance of certain words or phrases in the data being downloaded (filtering).

Neither of these approaches is foolproof. Remember, the web is a dynamic place with content being added, changed, and deleted from all over the world during every second of every day. No person, organization, or robot could ever document all websites at any given moment which might contain objectionable material. In trying, some legitimate websites are also screened out based on the occurrence of certain words or phrases that could very well be written in a daily newspaper or even the Bible. One of my own websites was blocked by schools because it provided information about confronting sexual harassment and contained words (probably "sex") that triggered the school's filters. Sometimes an Internet filter will allow a picture from a pornographic site to appear in the browser before triggering a block. This is because many porn sites purposely represent all the "words" in the opening page in the form of graphics in order to defeat any word filter. And, of course, once a picture is on the computer screen it can be saved, printed, e-mailed, or posted just about anywhere else on the Net before it is eventually discovered and added to the blocking list which means that the photo can be found elsewhere, namely some kid's cell phone or e-mail.

So, although blocking/filtering software is not foolproof and you should not completely rely on them, you should use them in conjunction with other measures. At my home we use *CyberSitter* (http://www.cybersitter.com) which I love. It does an excellent job of blocking, is easily customizable, and is jam packed with lots of helpful features. With CyberSitter, you can:

GuardingKids.com

- Block access to undesirable web sites. Over 35 filter categories are provided;
- Record and view all web sites visited;
- Record both sides of chat conversations from AOL Instant Messenger, Yahoo Messenger, and MSN Messenger;
- Block or limit access to popular but potentially dangerous services such as MySpace and FaceBook;
- Set time restrictions for internet usage;
- Get activity reports by e-mail;
- Configure the program via remote control.

Other popular blocking/filtering software resources include:

- America On Line (AOL) has created features to help parents make sure their children have a fun and enriching experience online, while limiting access to some features of AOL and the Internet. These "Parental Controls" allow parents to designate different levels of access for each child. http://www.aol.com. Also, MSN has a fully featured parental control as well. http://www.msn.com
- Many schools and libraries incorporate Bess filtering software which you may want to learn more about. http://www.securecomputing.com/index.cfm?skey=1209
- Cyber Patrol is used to manage Internet access, limit the total time spent online and restrict access to Internet sites that you deem inappropriate. http://www.cyberpatrol.com
- Cyber Sentinel allows user to block inappropriate material (web pages, e-mail, pictures, and word processing documents) no matter what format it is in, or what it is. It also allows the owner to configure the program to run in stealth mode (so the end user doesn't know it is running). The owner can then run Cyber Sentinel later and see screen shots of when the user was viewing inappropriate material. http://www.securitysoft.com/
- Net Nanny allows you to monitor, screen and block access to anything residing on, or running in your PC, whether you are connected to the Internet or not, and in real time. http://www.netnanny.com
- Mac users will want check out Content Barrier (http://www.intego.com/contentbarrier/) and Kids GoGoGo (http://www.makienterprise.com).
- K9 Web Protection, for both Windows and Macintosh, is a free Internet filtering and control solution for the home. http://www1.k9webprotection.com/
- The parental controls built into Windows Vista are designed to help parents manage what their children can do on the computer. These controls help parents determine which games their children can play, which programs they can use, and which websites they can visit—and when. http://tinyurl.com/39xefv
- For very young computer users, I like FreeShield which provides very good parental controls. In addition to blocking sites with adult content or content that would not be appropriate for children, FreeShield allows you to simply create and update lists of "good" sites and "bad" sites, the latter of which get completely blocked. http://www.freeshield.com/

Keylogging

Keylogging software is much more aggressive than monitoring software because it actually registers or records every keystroke a user types. This type of software has been traditionally used by online attackers who secretly plant the keylogging software on your computer and then analyze the data for passwords or other information they can use. Businesses and organizations use this type of software to snoop on their workers, especially to determine breaches in confidentiality that could compromise trade secrets. Keylogging software has found a new home inside the homes of parents because they allow you to have access to and read chat discussions, e-mails, passwords, and other online activity eminating from your personal computer. Screen captures (snapshots of the screens in the form of a graphic file) are also typically recorded at specified time intervals so you can see exactly what your child sees. Most keyloggers run in the background and are very difficult to circumvent or disable. Check out these to get you started:

IamBigBrother. http://www.iambigbrother.com

PC Tattletale http://www.pctattletale.com

eBlaster http://www.spectorsoft.com

Snoopstick. This one is from the same makers of CyberSitter. http://www.snoopstick.com/

Guardian Monitor Pro http://www.guardiansoftware.com/index2.html

For Apple Macintosh® users, you will be glad to know that there is a version of Spector for Macs as well. http://www.spectorsoft.com

Other Ways to Filter/Block Sites

Parental Controls on your Browser

To help keep kids safer online, parents can control browsing behavior through the parental control settings built into their web broswer such as with Internet Explorer 7. The child's safety level can be monitored and changed remotely. The safety level carries over to many PC activities, such as playing games or browsing the Internet. A child's browsing session can even be examined by a parent afterwards, and cannot be removed without the parent's permission. Check the settings for the broswer you are using to see what type of parental controls are available. You can also do a web search using the keywords "parental control" (without quotes) and the name of the browser you are using. Realize, however, that more than just one browser exists. So if your child doesn't like what you've done with one, he can download another for free.

Using Your Router

More homes are now using Internet routers to distribute their Internet connections among two or more computers. Wireless routers allow you to do this without using hard wire connections. If you have a high-speed connection, your network router may offer some stronger domain blocking features. Since every router is different, I can't provide precise instructions for how to setup domain blocking with your particular model so check with your manual or the company's other technical support.

GuardingKids.com

Child/Family Friendly Internet Service Providers

Some Internet Service Providers (ISP; e.g., http://www.integrityonline.com and http://www.cleanweb.net) have automatic controls of content, both web and e-mail, before it is even allowed to enter your computer. Given hundreds or thousands of dial-up numbers, you can have filtered web surfing and e-mail correspondence from throughout the country. When using a filtered ISP, you typically do not have to worry about keeping your filtering or blocking software updated because the filtering occurs at the ISP provider level, not at your computer. If you live in an area where a company does not have coverage, or would like to stick to your cable, DSL or broadband service provider, you may still be able to filter through a Family Friendly ISP proxy connection or similar service. Other family friendly ISP's include:

http://www.characterlink.net/

http://www.711online.net/

http://www.viafamily.com/

http://www.Safeplace.net can filter existing service with your current ISP. This includes DSL and Cable access, and will protect all computers in a single family residential access network.

Bookmarking

You may decide to allow your children to only access pre-approved (by you) sites which can be accessed by clicking on a bookmark or shortcut. This can work especially for young children who would not have the patience to type in a website address or URL anyway. So, after you decided that a site is okay, put a button or bookmark on that site and instruct children to navigate the web by using *only* the buttons or bookmark links. There are three ways to do this, you can do one or more:

1. Choose your child's favorite site as a homepage which is the page that automatically opens up after launching a browser. You can easily change the home page by dragging the little graphical icon next to the web address to the browsers icon for homepage, usually an icon depicting a house. For Microsoft Internet Explorer, check out a nice online tutorial for doing this at http://www.mistupid.com/technical/homepage/.

2. Create a special folder in your Bookmarks or Favorites and add only approved sites to that folder.

3. You can create your own web page of approved sites and make this your home page so your child sees it as soon as the browser is opened (or he/she can easily navigate to it just by clicking on the "house" icon on the browser). The easiest way to create your own home page of approved sites is to use a free online bookmark service which can be updated from any computer with Internet access. Here are a few popular ones to consider:

   – Yahoo! Bookmarks (http://bookmarks.yahoo.com/),

   – MyBookmarks (http://www.mybookmarks.com/)

   – Google Bookmarks (http://www.google.com/bookmarks/)

   – del.icio.us (http://del.icio.us/)

Typically, Your Internet Explorer favorites, Netscape bookmarks, and AOL favorite places can be imported to these online bookmarking services to get started quickly. The primary advantage of doing an online bookmark page is that you can let others such as family members or relatives know about it and share/swap sites for review and approval.

Limited User Accounts

In Windows XP Home Edition and Vista, there are two basic types of local user accounts (in addition to the guest account): administrators and limited users. [106] Setting up a limited user account (LUA) for each of your children has several advantages. First, a limited user cannot make major changes to the system including the installation of unwanted software without approveal by you, the "administrator." This is also useful from a security standpoint because if someone logged into a limited user account accidentally downloads malicious software designed to significantly alter your computer, it will probably be prohibited by this type of account. Secondly, your administrator account and your children's limited user accounts are separately maintained and only accessible with the appropriate passwords. In other words, they can't get into your stuff! (Although you, as the administrator, can get into theirs if you wish). The only disadvantage of the LUA is that, every now and then, a piece of software may not run if it rely's on a file that is outside the access rights of the LUA. When this happens, though, you can often fix it by reinstalling the software and checking off "all users." A word of caution ... like everything else, there is available online software to get around this, essentially elevating a LUA to administrator level with all rights and priviliges (e.g., MakeMeAdmin; see http://blogs.msdn.com/aaron_margosis/archive/2004/07/24/193721.aspx)

A Few Words about Proxy Servers

Think of your computer (or school computers for that matter) with Internet filters or blocking programs as a telephone that can dial only a few numbers. However, one of those numbers belongs to a friend who can start a conference call with anyone else in the world. That friend is the proxy. [107] A proxy server is a kind of buffer between your computer and the Internet resources you are accessing. The data you request come to the proxy first, and only then it transmits the data to you. This is how some children are getting around filters and blockers (and how some adults anonymously shop or gamble online while at work without being detected). Getting to a proxy server is not that difficult, at least for some kids. There are available online lists of free proxy servers that one can use to surf the Internet without restrictions. For instance, a popular one called SpySurfing (http://www.spysurfing.com/), has this as the very first line on their website:

Unblock MySpace - If your school blocks the popular website MySpace.com you can get around that and unblock MySpace using our proxy service!

There are other free proxy servers which continue to operate because they are supported by advertisement, one of which is even dedicated to unblocking MySpace (http://unblockMySpace.com/). And, if a kid wanted to set up their own home computer as a proxy, there is free software available online for him/her to do just that (in about 3 easy steps). One website even provides a program that purports to "get around all web blocking programs." The only caveat that this website provides is that "*You don't actually install the (program name deleted) on the computer that is blocked from accessing Websites. You, or a friend of yours, has to install the (program) on some other machine which is not censored.*"

One thing you might want to try is to test the integrity of your filtering/blocking software against known online proxy servers. For instance, go to http://www.anonymouse.org and try to access websites that normally are blocked or filtered. Are they still being blocked or filtered?

Computer Security

Pornography and other nefarious code may be distributed by others in the form of hidden viruses, malware, trojan horses and other nasty delivery methods. Whether you're a kid, adult, or somewhere in between, it is excellent practice to keep your computer safe/secure from outside threats. Remember, nobody is completely immune from catching a computer virus, becoming victim to a phishing scam, or being the target of a clever piece of spyware unless one practices technology or computing abstinence. To completely avoid computers, the Internet, and, to an increasing degree, gadgets such as cell phones, PDA's, and mp3 players is not an option in today's high-tech world. You can, however, significantly lower your risk by taking some precautions. I have online available for you a brief guide to maintaining a secure computer at http://www.schoolcounselor.com/resources/computer-security.htm

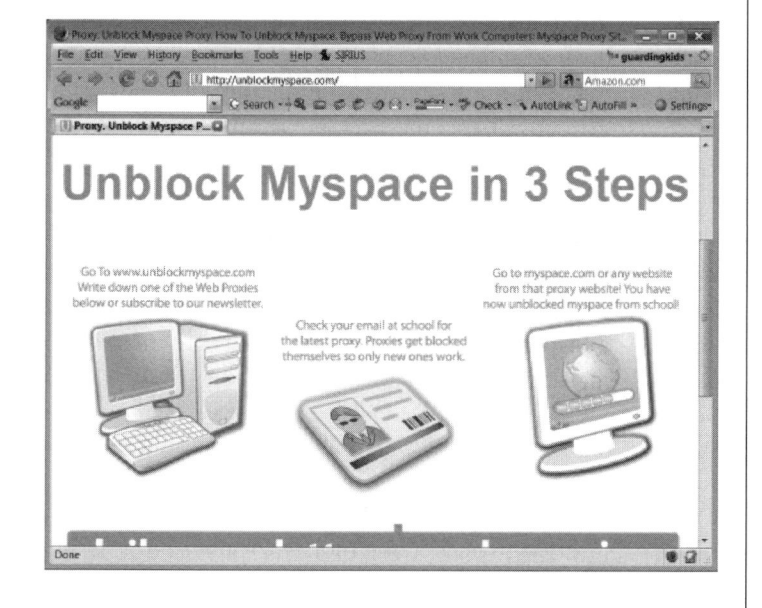

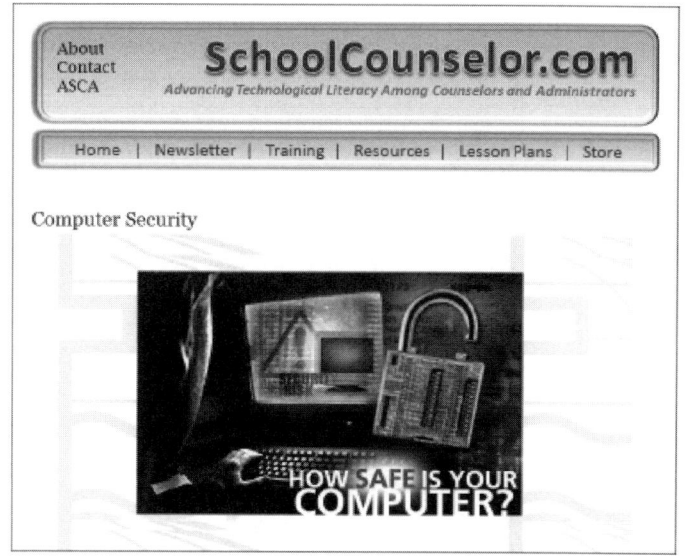

Summary

Technology provides us with tools to help us accomplish our work more effectively and efficiently beyond what we can do without it. Computers, cell phones, gaming devices, iPods, and other gadgets help us to stay connected, have fun, and better learn. Such power, however, comes with great responsibility and sometimes at a premium price. We must all make certain that we are using high-tech tools responsibly for ourselves and our society. We must ensure that our children understand how to emrace the tools of the 21st century in a manner that is safe and secure. Technological literacy for adults and children alike will help us to make decisions that are right and realistic. It is important that we each make a personal committment and take the time to evaluate the use and impact of technology in the lives of our families. Then, with great care, it is critical that we appropriately learn, teach, monitor, and supervise so that we may appropriately guard our kids from high-tech trouble.

With technology, we can do many things. However, just because we can, doesn't mean we should.

Resourceful Websites

The following websites can be very helpful in learning more about personal technology safety and for teaching caretakers about how to better guard kids from high-tech trouble. Many of these resources include lesson plans that can be incorporated into classroom guidance, parent consultation, and peer helper training.

2 SMRT 4U

http://www.2-smrt-4u.com/

U.S. Postal Inspection Service and the National Center for Missing and Exploited Children join together to launch 2 SMRT 4U Internet Safety Campaign, an effort to encourage teens to practice safe, smart habits when posting information about themselves on social networking web sites and blogs.

A Byte-Size Online Safety Guide

http://www.nick.com/blab/safety/index.jhtml

Excellent info in a kid-friendly interface from the folks at Nickelodeon TV.

Addressing CyberBullying in Schools

http://www.wtvi.com/teks/06_07_articles/cyberbullying.html

On November 1, 2006, a panel of educators addressed issues of bullying and cyberbullying at the Oklahoma "Safe and Healthy Schools" conference sponsored by the Oklahoma State Department of Education. As a result, this site has ten specific suggestions for educators and school district leaders to effectively address bullying and cyberbullying which emerged as a result of this panel discussion.

A Parent's Guide to Internet Safety

http://www.fbi.gov/publications/pguide/pguidee.htm

From the Federal Bureau of Investigation Crimes Against Children Program.

AOL@SCHOOL

http://www.aolatschool.com/

AOL@SCHOOL provides educator-reviewed classroom resources for K-12 students and teachers in math, science, language arts, social studies and more. Here you can quickly find activities, research materials, educational games, multimedia resources and lesson plans for primary, elementary, middle and high school classes.

Association of Sites Advocating Child Protection (ASACP)

http://www.asacp.org/

Founded in 1996, the Association of Sites Advocating Child Protection (ASACP) is a non-profit organization dedicated to eliminating child pornography from the Internet. ASACP battles child pornography through its CP reporting hotline, and by organizing the efforts of the online adult industry to combat the heinous crime of child sexual abuse.

bNetS@vvy

http://bnetsavvy.com/

bNetS@vvy is a bimonthly e-newsletter offering parents, guardians, and teachers tools to help kids ages 9 to 14 stay safer online. It is published in partnership by the National Education Association Health Information Network, the National Center for Missing & Exploited Children and Sprint's Project Connect.

Bullying Resources from the AMA

http://www.ama-assn.org/ama/pub/category/2285.html

Bullying Awareness Week

http://www.bullyingawarenessweek.org/

Bullying Awareness Week is an opportunity for people at the grassroots level in communities around the world to get involved in this issue, not by waiting for "Someone else" to do something, but rather for us to work together on preventing bullying in our communities through education and awareness.

Child Safety on the Information Highway

http://www.safekids.com/child_safety.htm

Originally published by Lawrence J. Magid for the National Center for Missing and Exploited Children.

Child Abuse Prevention Services (CAPS)

http://www.kidsafe-caps.org/

Child Abuse Prevention Services (CAPS) is a not for profit, volunteer organization founded in 1982 to respond to the growing problem of child abuse and neglect on Long Island, New York. In 1995 CAPS created the Child Safety Institute, providing innovative and comprehensive child safety and child prevention programs and materials.

Child Safety from Microsoft

http://www.microsoft.com/protect/family/guidelines/

Whether your kids go online to browse, research school projects, play games, or chat with friends, you can help to keep them safer while they explore online with these articles and tips.

Children and the Internet: Laws Relating to Filtering, Blocking

http://www.ncsl.org/programs/lis/cip/filterlaws.htm

Laws relating to filtering, blocking and usage policies in schools and libraries.

Children and the Internet (Free PDF Brochure)

http://www.parentingpress.com/brochure/internet.pdf

Communities Can Stop Bullying

http://www.highmarkhealthyhigh5.com/mainBullying/index.shtml

Bullying can take on many forms: emotional, physical, verbal, sexual, racist and cyber (spreading hurtful rumors and/or images across electronic platforms). Kids that are victims of bullies may become depressed, anxious and develop low self-esteem. They will suddenly not want to go to school, where most bullying takes place. A school bus ride, a trip to their locker, recess or lunchtime may become a fearful part of their daily school life. And sadly, there is little being done to address this issue.

Crimes against Children Research Center (CCRC)

http://www.unh.edu/ccrc/

The mission of the Crimes against Children Research Center (CCRC) is to combat crimes against children by providing high quality research and statistics to the public, policy makers, law enforcement personnel, and other child welfare practitioners. CCRC is concerned with research about the nature of crimes including child abduction, homicide, rape, assault, and physical and sexual abuse as well as their impact.

Cyberbullying: Instant Cruelty (PDF)

http://www.mindoh.com/docs/FamilyActivity_CyberBullying.pdf

Your children will explore the ramifications of cyberbullying and examine the values that can prevent it.

Cyberbullying: Not Just Name-Calling

http://tinyurl.com/38e3lq

Harassment and humiliation take on new forms in Cyberspace. Learn about the consequences, actions and reactions of using cell phones, the Internet and other digital devices to bully ones peers.

Cyberbullying Presentation (PDF)

http://www.seattleschools.org/area/source/cyberbullying2007.pdf

This would make a great handout or guide for presenting.

Cyberbullying

http://www.cyberbullying.us/

A central repository and information clearinghouse for the phenomenon of cyberbullying. To note, cyberbullying is also called "cyber bullying," "electronic bullying," "e-bullying," "sms bullying," "mobile bullying," "online bullying," "digital bullying," or "Internet bullying." Here we will make available the latest news and headlines, and provide research findings, press releases, reports, and a number of useful resources and materials to assist those in positions that directly or indirectly deal with this problem.

Cyberbullying: Bullying with Technologies

http://tinyurl.com/2nqoxx

Today's news often warns of dangers on the Internet, and recent news stories relate cases of how kids are being nasty, or worse, to each other online. To be sure, there are bullies online, just like there are in everyday life. These bullies may be classmates of your children, kids in the community, people your children have never actually met, or your own children. What they've learned to do is to use technologies such as the Internet and cell phones to hurt the feelings of others. Visit this site to read more ...

GuardingKids.com

Cyberbullying

http://cyberbully.org/

Cyberbully.org is provided by the Center for Safe and Responsible Internet Use. CSRUI provides resources for educators and others to promote the safe and responsible use of the Internet.

CyberNetiquette Comix

http://disney.go.com/cybersafety/

An entertaining, interactive way for families to learn valuable lessons about online safety. Join classic Disney characters for adventure, fun, and online awareness tips. We encourage parents and children to enjoy and discuss these interactive fables together.

Cybersafety

http://www.ctap4.org/cybersafety/

Cybersafety is the safe and responsible use of the Internet and all information and communication technology devices, including mobile phones, digital cameras, and webcams. CTAP Region IV has crafted several resources for download at the right including a classroom poster on Cybersafety funded by AT&T Education, a PowerPoint presentation to accompany the poster, and other workshop handouts. Click on the buttons below for carefully selected and annotated resources in each of the six CyberSafety areas.

CyberSafety for Kids Online: A Parents' Guide (PDF)

http://www.ncpc.org/cms/cms-upload/ncpc/files/chcyber.pdf

From the National Crime Prevention Council.

CyberSafety.us: Internet Safety Rules for Kids

http://www.cybersafety.us/

The Internet is a great information resource, and also a great communication resource. Allowing people to talk to their friends, make new friends, and find people with similar interests from all over the world. Utilizing chat programs (like MSN Messenger, AIM, ICQ), chat rooms, forums, and a variety of other ways. However, it is important to remember when chatting online with somebody, that you never know who they really are. People often pretend to be someone they are not during casual relationships online. This site includes eight safety rules that kids should follow when on the web.

CyberSkill Development

http://www.cybersmartcurriculum.org/lesson_plans/

From the website: The CyberSmart! Education Company is dedicated to teaching secure, responsible and effective Internet and computer use. We are a national leader calling for a nationwide commitment and coordinated action agenda to teach cyber skills in order to build the social foundation and culture of secure computing in the 21st century. We provide free curriculum for American's 54 million school children and related fee-based training resources for K-12 administrators, technology leaders, librarians, media specialists, classroom teachers, parents and cyber security awareness training for Fortune 1000 enterprise employees.

CyberSmart Lesson Plans and Activity Sheets

http://www.cybersmartcurriculum.org/lesson_plans/index.asp?menu_type=con

The CyberSmart! Education Company is dedicated to teaching secure, responsible and effective Internet and computer use. They are a national leader calling for a nationwide commitment and coordinated action agenda to teach cyber skills in order to build the social foundation and culture of secure computing in the 21st century.

Dealing with Online Bullies

http://cybersmartcurriculum.org/lesson_plans/68_04.asp

Students reflect on the rewards of cyberspace and then consider bullying scenarios in which they examine their personal comfort levels. They learn to recognize such feelings and responsibly handle the unacceptable behavior of others.

Digital Safety Podcasts from Digital Smarts Blog by Power to Learn

http://www.commonsensemedia.org/news/podcast.php

Would you like to know more about what the experts are saying about media and kids and digital safety but don't have time to read about it? One solution is the podcasts from Common Sense Media. The topics covered include everything from Using the TV as a Nanny to Smoking in the Movies and Kids' Health.

Don't Believe the Type

http://tcs.cybertipline.com/

This information was adapted from Teen Safety on the Information Highway written by Lawrence J. Magid, a syndicated columnist, media commentator, and host of www.safekids.com and www.safeteens.com.

GetNetWise

http://www.getnetwise.org/

The Internet is an increasingly important place to work, play and learn for both adults and children. At the same time, we are concerned about the risks we face online. The challenge is to stay "one-click" ahead of would-be pornographers, hackers, child-predators and those who would misuse your and your child's sensitive information. GetNetWise can help.

How to Setup and Use the Windows Vista Parental Controls

http://tinyurl.com/349mu7

This website provides a step-by-step tutorial with screenshots.

How Parents Can Block Certain Websites from Children at Home

http://www.labnol.org/software/browsers/block-websites-from-kids-home-computer/1602/

For non-techie parents who have a computer at home and are worried about their kids safety online.

i-SAFE America

http://www.isafe.org/

i-SAFE is a non-profit foundation dedicated to protecting the online experiences of youth everywhere. i-SAFE incorporates classroom curriculum with dynamic community outreach to empower students, teachers, parents, law enforcement, and concerned adults to make the Internet a safer place.

InSafe

http://www.saferinternet.org/

The mission of the Insafe cooperation network is to empower citizens to use the Internet, as well as other information and communication technologies, safely and effectively.

Instant Messaging, Chat Rooms, ICQ - Do You Know Who Your Kid's Talking To?

http://da.co.la.ca.us/pok/im.htm

Discusses protecting your child in an IM world.

GuardingKids.com

Internet Safety Sites from Teachers First

http://www.teachersfirst.com/safety.cfm

Links to a variety of curriculum categorized by appropriate grade level.

Internet Safety BLOG

http://internetsafetyadvisor.squarespace.com/

A resourceful blog about Internet Safety from Jace Shoemaker-Galloway, Internet Safety Coordinator, Macomb Online Safety Team (M.O.S.T.) Chairperson

Internet Content Rating Association

http://www.icra.org/

The Internet Content Rating Association is an independent, non-profit organization whose mission is to protect children from potentially harmful material.

Internet Crime Complaint Center (IC3)

http://www.ic3.gov/

The Internet Crime Complaint Center (IC3) is a partnership between the Federal Bureau of Investigation (FBI) and the National White Collar Crime Center (NW3C). IC3's mission is to serve as a vehicle to receive, develop, and refer criminal complaints regarding the rapidly expanding arena of cyber crime. The IC3 gives the victims of cyber crime a convenient and easy-to-use reporting mechanism that alerts authorities of suspected criminal or civil violations. For law enforcement and regulatory agencies at the federal, state, local and international level, IC3 provides a central referral mechanism for complaints involving Internet related crimes.

Internet Superheroes

http://www.internetsuperheroes.com/

Delivering smart, safe and responsible surfing messages to children, teens, schools and parents, online and offline.

Internet Safety: What You Don't Know Can Hurt Your Child

http://www.ncsbi.gov/icac/icac_parents_safetyvideo.jsp

To help you learn about the dangers of the Internet and how to protect your children, the North Carolina Department of Justice produced a video "Internet Safety: What You Don't Know Can Hurt Your Child" and a companion resource guide.

Internet Keep Safe Coalition at iKeepSafe.org

http://www.ikeepsafe.org/

The Internet Keep Safe Coalition group teaches basic rules of Internet safety to children and parents, reaching them online and in school. Governors and/or first spouses formed this coalition in partnership with a growing list of crime prevention organizations, law enforcement agencies, foundations and corporate sponsors.

Internet Safety for Teachers

http://www.safekids.ne.gov/teachers.html

As educators you play a vital role in not only helping students understand the Internet, but also in educating them on the dangers that lurk online. Here you will find free interactive lessons you can use in your classroom.

Internet Safety: Parents and Guardians

http://www.ncsbi.gov/icac/icac_parents.jsp

To learn how to keep your children safer, watch the video "Internet Safety: What You Don't Know Can Hurt Your Child" and get a copy of the accompanying resource guide. Use the resource guide, and check this website for updates about new developments like MySpace.

GuardingKids.com

Internet Crimes Against Children (ICAC) Program

http://www.icactraining.org/

The ICAC Task Force Program was created to help State and local law enforcement agencies enhance their investigative response to offenders who use the Internet, online communication systems, or other computer technology to sexually exploit children. The program is currently composed of 45 regional Task Force agencies and is funded by the United States Office Of Juvenile Justice and Delinquency Prevention. The Training & Technical Assistance Program was established to assist these agencies with training and technical assistance in support of their Internet Crimes Against Children initiatives.

Internet Smarts

http://www.powertolearn.com/internet_smarts/parents_need_to_know/index.shtml

Designed to provide parents with timely and relevant information related to children's digital media safety these interactive units provide in-depth, practical and "how to" information.

Kidsmart

http://www.kidsmart.org.uk/

Kidsmart is an award winning practical internet safety programme website for schools, young people, parents, and agencies, produced by the children's internet charity Childnet International.

Know Your Computer Lingo

http://www.alliancecom.net/internet_lingo.php

A comprehensive list of acronyms and what they mean.

Let's Fight it Together: A Cyberbullying Film

http://www.digizen.org/cyberbullying/fullFilm.aspx

Also comes with a teacher's guide.

Linda Thomas at the Movies

http://www.lindathomasmovies.com/

Excellent movie reviews and ratings to check out before watching them with the kids.

MailFrontier Field Guide to Phishing (PDF)

http://www.mailfrontier.com/docs/field_guide.pdf

With the MailFrontier" Field Guide to Phishing", you'll find clear, concise explanations and visual representations of sneaky, dangerous phish that may find their way to your computer. To help you identify these nasty threats – and trust your other incoming mail – at the end of this field guide are some suggestions on how you can protect yourself, as well as other phishing resources for more information."

McGruff Kid Safe Software

http://www.mcgruffbrowser.com/

Claim your FREE McGruff the Crime Dog Kid Safe Browser today!

Michigan Model Bully Prevention

http://www.emc.cmich.edu/CORE/bully.htm

The Michigan Model is a comprehensive curriculum. Each grade level includes activities and lessons that teach students skills for dealing with bullying situations. To aid in locating these lessons, the following chart is provided. Lesson links will take you to teacher pages for specific lessons.

Microsoft Protect Your Family Page

http://tinyurl.com/2tr7mk

Did you upgrade to Windows Vista or are you thinking about it? If so you'll want to check out the information about family safety features - monitoring usage, setting time limits, and controlling access to websites, programs, and games by individual family member - in the latest Windows operating system.

Mirror Image

http://www.wiredwithwisdom.org/

Mirror Image is a detective-style computer game that teaches teens to be safe in online chat rooms by challenging players to outsmart a cyber stalker. The game is based on a real-life criminal case involving cyber stalking. The game has been designed for students to use in a classroom, guided by a teacher or a police officer and can be completed in one class period.

National Institute on Media and the Family

http://www.mediafamily.org/

The National Institute on Media and the Family is the world's leading and most respected research-based organization on the positive and harmful effects of media on children and youth.

NetAlert SafeSchools

http://www.netalert.net.au/03711-CyberSafe-Schools.asp

NetAlert SafeSchools provides a host of materials for teachers interested in tackling Internet safety with their students. It's a great site to tell parents about also. The content includes resources for secondary and primary school students along with professional teacher materials. Cartoon lessons and downloadable materials are available. There's also a CyberSafe newsletter featuring the latest in Internet safety projects.

NetBullies.com

http://www.netbullies.com/pages/1/index.htm

Useful information and links.

NetSmartz

http://www.netsmartz.org/

The NetSmartz Workshop is an interactive, educational safety resource that teaches kids and teens how to stay safer on the Internet. NetSmartz combines the newest technologies available and the most current information to create high-impact educational activities that are well received by even the most tech-savvy kids. Parents, guardians, educators, and law enforcement also have access to additional resources for learning and teaching about the dangers children may face online. NetSmartz was created by the National Center for Missing & Exploited Childrenr (NCMEC) and Boys & Girls Clubs of America (BGCA).

OnGuardOnline.gov

http://onguardonline.gov/

OnGuardOnline.gov provides practical tips from the federal government and the technology industry to help you be on guard against Internet fraud, secure your computer, and protect your personal information.

Online Sexual Exploitation Campaign from the Ad Council

http://www.adcouncil.org/default.aspx?id=56

The Internet has helped to enrich our lives in many ways, however, it has also provided child predators with a new way to reach potential victims and commit crimes. This page has excellent resources you can use to help prevent this tragic issue.

GuardingKids.com

Online-Safety Resources for Home & School

http://www.netfamilynews.org/resourcesphishing.htm

Have you gotten an email from PayPal, eBay, Citibank, or even your own bank lately? Did it say something unnerving about a certain amount having been removed from your account, or you can't use your account until you update it - "click here to update"? Chances are, it's a phishing scam.

Parenting with Technology

http://www.powertolearn.com/articles/parenting_with_technology/

Informative and timely articles.

Parents Guide to the Information Superhighway

http://www.childrenspartnership.org/bbar/pbpg.html

It's designed to welcome you, and give you a simple step-by-step introduction to parenting in a world of computers and new forms of media. This Guide will provide some tools and rules for you to use with your children at home, at school, and in the community. Also in Spanish.

Point Smart. Click Safe.

http://www.pointsmartclicksafe.org/

Today's kids know how to use the technology, but do they understand Internet safety concerns, cyber ethical dilemmas and how to think critically about the media and technology they use? Point Smart. Click Safe., a new cable initiative, helps you teach them how to be smart, safe and savvy in the digital world.

Protect Yourself from Internet Harassment and Stalking

http://castlecops.com/article-5427-nested-0-0.html

This article, written by Larry Stevenson, includes a checklist to protect yourself from harassment and stalkers while online.

Resources for Bully Prevention and Intervention

http://www.fcps.net/sa/support/bully/resources.htm

Resources for bully prevention and intervention.

SafeSurf

http://www.safesurf.com/

SafeSurf is an organization dedicated to making the Internet safe for your children without censorship. They are developing and are implementing an Internet Rating Standard that is bringing together parents, providers, publishers, developers, and all the resources available on the Internet to achieve this goal. It involves marking sites with the SafeSurf Wave.

Six Ways to Be a Media-Savvy Parent This Year

http://tinyurl.com/2vbckv

If you've told yourself that this year you REALLY are going to get caught up to your kids when it comes to digital savvy, you might want to start by looking at the checklist on the Common Sense Media site of six ways to get started.

Stoptextbully.com

http://www.stoptextbully.com/

Mobile phones are great - you can stay in touch with your mates, chat to new friends, and have fun with cool ringtones, photos and video clips. But text bullies can use mobiles to get at you any time.

GuardingKids.com

Take a Stand. Lend a Hand. Stop Bullying Now!

http://www.stopbullyingnow.hrsa.gov/

The U.S. Department of Health and Human Services, the Health Resources and Services Administration, and the Maternal and Child Health Bureau created this awesome place for us to go to get the latest scoop on bullying.

TeachersFirst Internet Safety Lesson Links

http://www.teachersfirst.com/safety.cfm

Do a lesson on Internet Safety using one of the resources from TeachersFirst and have students make web safety posters, PowerPoints, or videos.

Teenangels

http://www.teenangels.org/

Teenangels is a group of 13-18 year-old volunteers that have been specially trained by the FBI, local law enforcement, and many other leading safety experts in all aspects of online safety, privacy, and security. After training for six sessions, the Teenangels run unique programs in schools to spread the word about responsible and safe surfing to other teens and younger kids, parents, and teachers. At the urging of our Teenangel volunteers, a special group of volunteers will be able to continue as Teenangels after they become 18 years old, & a new group of Tweenangels has been formed for those between 11 & 13 years of age.

Test your MySpace Safety Knowledge

http://www.komando.com/myspace/

Kids love the social-networking Web site MySpace.com. But far too often, their profiles disclose too much personal information. See if your child can spot 10 safety problems in the sample MySpace page. You may have to scroll down to view all of the safety issues. Then, follow the links below the profile to see if your child is correct!

The National Cyber Security Alliance

http://www.staysafeonline.info

A not-for-profit 501(c)(3) organization, the National Cyber Security Alliance (NCSA) is the go-to resource for cyber security awareness and education for home user, small business, and education audiences.

The Computer & Chat Lingo Links

http://www.city-net.com/~ched/help/lingo/jargonlinks.html

Lots of computer and chat room slang/lingo.

TheParentsEdge

http://www.theparentsedge.com/

Giving parents the tools and resources they need to keep their kids safe online. Free guides, how-to's and resources to help parents deal with myspace and online predators.

Web Wise Kids

http://www.webwisekids.com/

Web Wise Kids is a non-profit organization dedicated to empowering today's youth to make wise choices online. WWK leads the way marrying education and technology to reach today's e-generation by using computer games to communicate Internet safety. High tech simulations based on real-life criminal cases prepare children to safely and confidently explore the cyber world capturing their attention in a way that "another lecture from an adult" can never do.

Wired Safety

http://www.wiredsafety.org/

WiredSafety.org is the home of WiredKids.org, WiredPatrol.org and Cyberlawenforcement.org (WiredCops.org). They provide four things: information, education, help and training for law enforcement. They help people of all ages with anything that can go wrong online, from con artists, identity thieves, predators, stalkers, criminal hackers, online fraud, cyber-romance gone wrong and privacy problems.

Wired Kids

http://www.wiredkids.com/

Wired Kids Inc, Inc is a 501(c)3, dedicated to protecting children from sexual exploitation related to the Internet.

Working to Halt Online Abuse (WHOA)

http://www.haltabuse.org

WHOA is a volunteer organization founded in 1997 to fight online harassment through education of the general public, education of law enforcement personnel, and empowerment of victims. They've also formulated voluntary policies which they encourage online communities to adopt in order to create safe and welcoming environments for all internet users.

Yahooligans! Parent Guide

http://yahooligans.yahoo.com/parents/

"Safe surfing" is a family affair. As a parent, it's all about being informed, Internet savvy, and open to the possibilities of the online world for you and your child. Check out this guide for parents from Yahoo!

Your Guide to Safe Surfing (PDF)

http://tinyurl.com/2wgy8g

Your Guide to Safe Surfing: Learning about the Internet is an instructional booklet geared toward middle school students in order to help them learn more about how to use the Internet safely, correctly, and ethically. It is written in the format of a guide for surfing and is themed accordingly. It is divided into three distinct sections: "Treading Water," "Standing up," and "Surfing."

Youth Violence and Electronic Media

http://www.jahonline.org/content/suppl07

In December 2007 the Centers for Disease Control and Prevention sponsored a supplement to the Journal of Adolescent Health and a list of resources on cyberbullying for parents, teachers and administrators is included. The title of the supplement was "Youth Violence and Electronic Media: Similar Behaviors, Different Venues?" and discusses the growing public health issue of the connection between Electronic Media, Violence, and Adolescents.

Endnotes

1. Tyler, J.M., & Sabella, R.A. (2004). Using technology to improve counseling practice: A primer for the 21st Century. Alexandria, VA: American Counseling Association.

2. Mendez, Z. (April 21, 2006). NJ student suspended over MySpace video. New Jersey Daily Record.

3. Adolescents' use of cell phones after bedtime contributes to poor sleep. (September 1, 2007). American Academy of Sleep Medicine. Available online: http://www.physorg.com/news107857517.html

4. Roebuck, J. (May 1, 2007). Teen arrested for Internet threats. The Monitor. Available online: http://www.themonitor.com/onset?id=2061&template=article.html

5. Associated Press. (November 2, 2005). Grandpa sued over grandson's downloads: 67-year-old man refuses $4,000 settlement offer. Available online: http://www.msnbc.msn.com/id/9896986/

6. Associated Press. (April 27, 2006). Girl home after running away with Myspace.com correspondent. Available online: http://tinyurl.com/2nm3je

7. Sutta, D. (May 8, 2006). Another suspect charged in child predator sting. Available online: http://www.nbc-2.com/articles/readarticle.asp?articleid=7000&z=3&p=

8. School Punishes Student For Blogging From Home. (May 25, 2006). Available online: http://rhymeswithright.mu.nu/archives/178392.php. Also, see the student's letter to the school district online at http://tinyurl.com/32ehuh

9. America's Most Wanted. (December 30, 2006). A new "Friend" online. Available online: http://www.amw.com/fugitives/case.cfm?id=38571

10. Williams, R. (January 16, 2008). Cellphone porn at school investigated. Roanoke Times. Available online: http://www.roanoke.com/news/roanoke/wb/147238

11. Associated Press. (January 7, 2008). Teacher accused of sending nude cell phone pics to student. Available online: http://tinyurl.com/3a3ztk

12. Mendels, P. (June 22, 1999). Hate groups target children and women online, report says. Available online: http://www.rickross.com/reference/hate_groups/hategroups39.html

13. Kornblum, J. (May 7, 2006). Text messages give '411' on teen sex. USA Today. Available online: http://tinyurl.com/2tq2h7

14. Warning over 'bullying by mobile'. (June 7, 2005). BBC News. Available online: http://news.bbc.co.uk/1/hi/education/4614515.stm

15. King, D. (August 11, 2005). Hot, steamy and now downloadable: Aural sex shimmies into the podcast as 'podnography' trend takes off. San Francisco Chronicle. Available online: http://www.sfgate.com/c/a/2005/08/11/DDGIHE5CTJ1.DTL

16. Kennedy, K. (April 23, 2006). Not-so-MySpace any more: Schools are banning popular social web site, prosecuting students' speech. The Ledger. Available online: http://tinyurl.com/2vhh6a

17. Josephson, M. (February 7, 2006). The parental authority to be involved. Los Angeles County District Attorney's Office. Available online: http://da.co.la.ca.us/pok/parentalcon.htm

18. Unites States Department of Justice PROTECT Act of 2003 Fact Sheet. (April 30, 2003). Available online: http://www.usdoj.gov/opa/pr/2003/April/03_ag_266.htm

19. Edelman, B. (February 18, 2003). Domains Reregistered for Distribution of Unrelated Content: a case study of "Tina's Free Live Webcam." Berkman Center for Internet & Society at Harvard Law School. Available online: http://cyber.law.harvard.edu/people/edelman/renewals/

20. Gutierrez T. and McCabe, K. (November 11, 2005). Parents: Online newsgroup helped daughter commit suicide: Online newsgroup members trade messages about suicide desires, methods. CNN. Available online: http://www.cnn.com/2005/US/11/04/suicide.internet/index.html

21. If you are a teacher or even a parent, you can find lesson plans about music downloading and copyright infringement by visiting http://www.readwritethink.org/lessons/lesson_view.asp?id=855

22. Markon, J. (August 26, 2006). Florida man gets six years in prison for software privacy. Washington Post. Available online: http://tinyurl.com/348ven

23. Hubbard, J. (August 29, 2006). Students punished for using computers inappropriately. RedOrbit. Available online: http://tinyurl.com/2wg4ys

24. Zolcer, S. (September 07, 2006). Fake exam certificates trade. Budapest Sun. Available online: http://www.budapestsun.com/cikk.php?id=12999

25. Greene, T. C. (January 29, 2005). Norwegian student fined for MP3 links. The Register. Available online: http://tinyurl.com/6ykes

26. Twohey, M. (Retrieved January 24, 2008). You've got lawsuit: Father sued for teen's downloads. Milwaukee Journal Sentinel. Available online: http://www.jsonline.com/story/index.aspx?id=326357

27. Avila, J. (February 19, 1999). High-tech cheating hits schools. ZDNet. Available online: http://news.zdnet.com/2100-9595_22-513776.html

28. High-tech Cheating Leads To Injuries. (June 20, 2006). ZDNet. Available online: http://news.zdnet.com/2100-1040_22-6085712.html

29. Hafner, K. (September 19, 2003). Is it wrong to share your music? (Discuss). New York Times. Available online: http://tinyurl.com/2wvft6

30. Parker, R. (November 7, 2005). High-tech options helping students cheat. The Arizona Republic. Available online: http://tinyurl.com/2re3t8

31. Cormier, A. (September 09. 2006). Honors students punished for plagiarism: Parents worry "mistakes" will tarnish reputations. Herald Tribune. Available online: http://tinyurl.com/2rjje2

32. Kendall, D. S. (Retrieved January 24, 2008). Nobody's going to check parenting and plagiarism. Power to Learn. Available online: http://tinyurl.com/2lghj8

33. Software cracking. (2008, January 24). In Wikipedia, The Free Encyclopedia. Retrieved 16:41. http://tinyurl.com/37hzpd

34. Pitterman, C. (Retrieved January 24, 2008). When your writing isn't your own: Get the lowdown with answers to commonly asked questions about. plagiarism. Available online: http://content.scholastic.com/browse/article.jsp?id=1604

35. For example, see http://tinyurl.com/2q9vno or http://www.campusdownloading.com/legal.htm

36. Justin Berry. (2008, January 20). In Wikipedia, The Free Encyclopedia. Retrieved 16:42, January 25, 2008, from http://tinyurl.com/3286yv. Also see Congressional Hearing Testimony of Justin Berry before the Investigations Subcommittee of the House Energy and Commerce Committee, April 4, 2006 at http://www.freecasey.com/transcripts/Eichenwald.pdf. Also know that the case of Mr. Berry is quite controversial and sparking some interesting debate online (e.g., see http://www.thetruthaboutjustin.com/).

37. cyber bullies: 10 signs of the player hater. (August 23, 2006). Vaspers the Great. http://tinyurl.com/3yxukt

38. Skype. (2008, January 24). In Wikipedia, The Free Encyclopedia. Retrieved 16:43, January 25, 2008, from http://tinyurl.com/2rrqv2

39. RSS. (2008, January 25). In Wikipedia, The Free Encyclopedia. Retrieved 16:44, January 25, 2008, from http://tinyurl.com/3ymv8z

40. For a more detailed explanation of podcasts, see Valesky, T. & Sabella, R.A. (2005). Podcasting in educational leadership and counseling. Paper presented at the conference of the Southern Regional Council on Educational Administration, Atlanta GA, October 28, 2005. Available online: http://coe.fgcu.edu/edleadership/podcasting.pdf

41. Also see List of social networking websites. (2008, January 24). In Wikipedia, The Free Encyclopedia. Retrieved 16:45, January 25, 2008, http://en.wikipedia.org/wiki/List_of_social_networking_sites and http://mashable.com/ to keep up with the daily evolution of social networking sites.

42. Kornblum, J. (October 30, 2005). Teens wear their hearts on their blog. Available online: http://tinyurl.com/75gwl

43. (Reprinted by permission). Robert J. Chapman, PhD Coordinator, AOD Program Associate Faculty, Clinical/Counseling Psychology La Salle University 1900 W. Olney Ave. Philadelphia, PA 19141-1199 Phone: 215-951-1357 Fax: 215-951-1451 chapman@lasalle.edu, http://www.robertchapman.net.

44. For more on AUP's see Acceptable Use Policies: A handbook from the Virginia Department of Education. Available online: http://www.doe.virginia.gov/VDOE/Technology/AUP/home.shtml

45. Take some time to review safety tips from Myspace.com by visiting http://tinyurl.com/32rfyj and the Xanga.com Cyber Bullying website at http://tinyurl.com/2sdlg3

46. Belsey, B. (2004). Always on, always aware. Available online: http://www.cyberbullying.ca/pdf/Cyberbullying_Information.pdf

47. Swartz, J. (March 7, 2005) Schoolyard bullies get nastier online. USA Today. Available online: http://tinyurl.com/ezu2f

48. Leishman, J. (March 2005). Cyber-bullying. CBS News Online. Available online: http://www.cbc.ca/news/background/bullying/cyber_bullying.html

49. http://www.jaredstory.com/bully.html . Also see http://www.jeffreyjohnston.org/.

50. Bamford, A. (2004). Cyber-Bullying. Available online: http://www.ahisa.com.au/documents/conferences/PCC2004/bamford.pdf.

51. For an excellent description of flaming via e-mail, I refer you to Dyrud, M.A. (2000). Flaming and thrashing: An examination of tone in electronic mail. Paper presented at the 30th ASEE/IEEE Frontiers in Education Conference. October 18 - 21, 2000 Kansas City, MO. Available online: http://fie.engrng.pitt.edu/fie2000/papers/1188.pdf

52. Bamford, A. (2004). Cyber-Bullying. Available online: http://www.ahisa.com.au/documents/conferences/PCC2004/bamford.pdf.

53. Bamford, A. (2004). Cyber-Bullying. Available online: http://www.ahisa.com.au/documents/conferences/PCC2004/bamford.pdf.

54. Blair, J. (2003). New breed of bullies torment their peers on the Internet. Education Week, Vol. 22 (21), p. 6-9.

55. Blair, J. (2003). New breed of bullies torment their peers on the Internet. Education Week, Vol. 22 (21), p. 6-9.

56. Partly adapted from Parents Need to be Aware that Bullying Has Gone Hi-Tech (March 9, 2006). Available online: http://tinyurl.com/35qj4q

57. Willard, N. E. (2007). Cyberbullying and cyberthreats: Responding to the challenge of online social aggression, threats, and distress. Champaign, Ill: Research Press. Note: You can read an in depth book review online at http://www.tpronline.org/book-review.cfm/Cyberbullying_and_Cyberthreats

58. Crawford, Krysten. (February 15, 2005). Have a blog, lose your job? Workers with web logs are everywhere, and they're starting to make corporate America very nervous. CNN/Money. Available online: http://money.cnn.com/2005/02/14/news/economy/blogging/

59. Cell phone GPS services are made possible through one's cellphone service provider or others such as http://www.catscommunication.com/, http://findme.mapquest.com/ or http://www.followus.co.uk/homeusers.html.

60. A killer application (commonly shortened to killer app), in the jargon of computer programmers and video gamers, has been used to refer to any computer program that is so necessary or desirable that it provides the core value of some larger technology, such as a gaming console, software, operating system, or piece of computer hardware. In this sense, a killer app substantially increases sales of the hardware that supports it. Source: Killer application. (2008, January 26). In Wikipedia, The Free Encyclopedia. Retrieved 20:05, January 27, 2008, from http://en.wikipedia.org/w/index.php?title=Killer_application&oldid=187089583

61. The survey was carried out by psychologists Nathalie Noret of York St. John University College and Ian Rivers, of Queen Margaret University College in Edinburgh. Source: London Entertainment Guide. (March 21, 2007). More falling prey to cyber-bullying. Available online: http://tinyurl.com/23za3x

62. DeMentri , V. (March 7, 2006). Text Messages Latest Tool For Child Predators. Available online: http://www.nbc10.com/investigatorsarchive/7792369/detail.html

63. Oglesby, C. (January 11, 2008). Cells, texting give predators secret path to kids. CNN. Available online: http://www.cnn.com/2008/CRIME/01/11/teachers.charged/

64. Kennedy, B. A. (April 23, 2007). Magic thumbs! 13-year-old wins text-messaging championship. Available online: http://tinyurl.com/2yq3sw

65. OUT-LAW.COM. (February 22, 2006). Millions suffer RSI' from text messaging: Xrcises 2 prolng yr txtin life. Available online: http://www.theregister.co.uk/2006/02/22/text_injury/.

66. Baggott, K. (December 21, 2006). Literacy and text messaging: How will the next generation read and write? Available online: http://www.technologyreview.com/Biztech/17927/

67. NHTSA Policy and FAQs on Cellular Phone Use While Driving. Available online: http://tinyurl.com/3adgct

68. Sullivan, B. (August 20, 2004). Cell phones and kids: Do they mix? Games, other new features give parents more to think about. MSNBC. Available online: http://www.msnbc.msn.com/id/5671445/

69. Mobile Games from Independent Online. Available online: http://www.iol.co.za/index.php?click_id=2987&tribe_id=20730

70. Cohen, J. & Langer, G. (Februrary 3, 2006). Poll: Rudeness In America, 2006: It's the #@%! Cell phones. ABCNews. Available online: http://abcnews.go.com/2020/print?id=1574155

71. Briody, D. (2000). The ten commandments of cell phone etiquette. InfoWorld. Available online: http://tinyurl.com/7wjfv

72. Brown, T. (January 26, 2006). Cell-phone sex; will it play in Peoria? Reuters. Available online: http://tinyurl.com/3b9ezk

73. The Internet Patrol. (December 17, 2004). CEO of Online Auction Company Arrested for Home Porn Listed on Site. Available online: http://tinyurl.com/35hkkn

74. Philo G. (1997). The media and mental distress. London: Longman Group United Kingdom.

75. Cumberbatch, G. (2004). Video Violence: Villain or Victim? A review of the research evidence concerning media violence and its effects in the real world with additional reference to video games. Available online: http://tinyurl.com/3xgyr4

76. Brief amici curiae of thirty-three media scholars in interactive digital software Ass'n, et Al. V. St. Louis County, et Al. (September 24, 2002). Available online: http://www.fepproject.org/courtbriefs/stlouis.html

77. Anderson, C. (2002). FAQs on violent video games and other media violence. Available online: http://tinyurl.com/anuj4

78. 2006 Essential facts about the computer and video game industry. Entertainment Software Association. Available online: http://tinyurl.com/gonbv

79. Dobnik, V. (April. 7, 2004). Surgeons may err less by playing video games: Three hours a week decreased mistakes. Associated Press. Available online: http://www.msnbc.msn.com/id/4685909/

80. (May 28, 2003). Video games 'good for you'. BBC News. Available online: http://news.bbc.co.uk/2/hi/technology/2943280.stm

81. Dance Dance Revolution. (2008, January 25). In Wikipedia, The Free Encyclopedia. Retrieved 16:40, January 25, 2008, from http://tinyurl.com/2k4597

82. Totilo, S. (January 25, 2006). West Virginia adds 'Dance Dance Revolution' to gym class. MTV Networks. Available online: http://tinyurl.com/8xft7

83. Schmidt, T. S. (February 1, 2007). Is the Wii Really Good for Your Health? Available online: http://tinyurl.com/325eqy

84. McClurg, P. A. and Chaille, C. (1987). "Computer games: Environments for developing spatial cognition?" Journal of Educational Computing Research, Vol. 3(11), pp. 95-111.

85. Hostetter, O. (October 23, 2006). Video games - The necessity of incorporating video games as part of constructivist learning. Available online: http://tinyurl.com/33nrdl

86. Clothier, J. (April 15, 2005). English teacher ahead of the game. CNN Available online: http://www.cnn.com/2005/TECH/04/15/spark.teaching/index.html

87. Steinkuehler, C.A. (2005). Cognition & learning in massively multiplayer online games: A critical approach. Unpublished dissertation. Available online: http://tinyurl.com/3dy86k

88. Steinkuehler, C.A. (2005). The new third place: Massively multiplayer online gaming in american youth culture. Available online: http://tinyurl.com/3ywmyo

89. For example, see Video Game Violence: The Savage Se7en, an article that "take a trip back in time and revisit seven of the most 'controversial' titles in video game history." http://www.gamestar.com/11_04/features/fea_savageseven.shtml. Also, see Digital Death: The 10 Best Video Game Kills Ever at http://www.games.net/features/108181_1.shtml.

90. Anderson, C. A. and Dill, K. E. (2000). Video games and aggressive thoughts, feelings, and behavior in the laboratory and in life. Journal of Personality and Social Psychology, Vol. 78(4), p. 772-790.

Gentile, D. A., Lynch, P. J., Linder, J. R., and Walsh, D. A. (2004). The effects of violent video game habits on adolescent hostility, aggressive behaviors, and school performance. Journal of Adolescence, 27, 5-22. Available online: http://tinyurl.com/3bnr5e. Also see other publications from Dr. Gentile at http://tinyurl.com/2vnqr6.

91. Carnagey, N.L., Anderson, C.A., & Bushman, B.J. (2007). The effect of video game violence on physiological desensitization to real-life. Journal of Experimental Social Psychology, Vol. 43 p. 489–496. Available online: http://tinyurl.com/3aedwb

92. There is evidence to suggest that people who watch violent television are more likely to play violent video games and that media violence in general is related to aggressive diagnoses. For examples see Kronenberg, et al. (2005). *Media violence exposure in aggressive and control adolescents: Differences in self and parent reported exposure to violence on television and video games.* Aggressive Behavior, Vol. 31, pages 201-216.

93. BBC News. (August 10, 2005). S Korean dies after games session. Available online: http://news.bbc.co.uk/1/hi/technology/4137782.stm

94. Brody, L. (August 19, 2006). Can you be a video-game "addict"? The Record. Available online: http://tinyurl.com/2j35ou

95. Thompson, S. H. (November 3, 2002). Clicking the habit. Tampa, FL: The Tampa Tribune.

96. Computer and Video Game Addiction Fact Sheet. National Institute on Media and the Family. Available online: http://www.mediafamily.org/facts/facts_gameaddiction.shtml.

97. Sanchez, L. M. . August 23, 2002. Violent Video Games and Operant Conditioning: Physical and Psychological Effects. Maxwell School. Available online: http://tinyurl.com/2jwhb2

98. National Institute on Media and the Family. Available online: http://www.mediaandthefamily.org

99. To learn more about schedules of reinforcement, use a web search engine with the phrase "operant conditioning." Visit http://chiron.valdosta.edu/whuitt/col/behsys/operant.html as one place to begin.

100. For more information about gaming addiction, check out *Computer and Video Game Addiction* from the National Institute on Media and the Family website at http://www.mediafamily.org/facts/facts_gameaddiction.shtml

101. Helpful Tips for Parents. Entertainment Software Rating Board. Available online: http://www.esrb.org/about/parents_tips.jsp

102. Noguchi, S. (August 21, 2006). Teens, young adults making profession out of pastime. San Jose Mercury News. Available online: http://hamptonroads.com/node/142201

103. Leetspeak: A parent's primer to computer slang: Understand how your kids communicate online. (March 7, 2006). Available online: http://www.microsoft.com/protect/computer/basics/netiquette.mspx

104. United States Department of Justice Project Safe Childhood Program, Part 3, pg. 17. Available online: http://www.projectsafechildhood.gov/part3.pdf. For a full table of contents, visit http://www.projectsafechildhood.gov/guide.htm

105. Check out http://www.pen.k12.va.us/VDOE/Technology/AUP/home.shtml for a detailed handbook about AUP's.

106. Shinder, D. (April 26, 2005). Increasing security with limited user accounts and restricted groups. Available online: http://tinyurl.com/pwuhz

107. Pinzer, M. I. (May 22, 2006) Schools, students match wits over Web access. The Miami Herald. Available online: http://tinyurl.com/374dh7